Discovering Plato

Discovering Plato

By ALEXANDRE KOYRÉ

TRANSLATED BY
LEONORA COHEN ROSENFIELD

COLUMBIA UNIVERSITY PRESS
NEW YORK AND LONDON

This book was originally published as Number 9 of the Columbia Studies in Philosophy and was edited under the Department of Philosophy, Columbia University.

Copyright © 1945 Columbia University Press
Columbia Paperback Edition 1960

Fourth printing and second Paperback printing 1968
Printed in the United States of America

Foreword

I FEEL a certain diffidence about writing a foreword to M. Koyré's admirable *Discovering Plato*. My hesitation comes partly from the fact that my words will only detain the reader from plunging at once into these brilliantly suggestive pages and that he will be detained from going on at once to read—or reread—Plato, which the perusal of M. Koyré's little book will inevitably prompt him to do. I am further constrained by the fact that M. Koyré, well known in France, ought really to need no presentation to American readers, for his book itself will be as fine and adequate an introduction to him as anyone could desire.

For M. Koyré has accomplished in this book a feat of scholarship and illumination peculiarly the gift of the French academic tradition. The book is short, but one has the impression after reading it that one has had the intellectual nutriment of a much longer work. The book is spirited and epigrammatic, but its incisiveness is clearly merely the index to a sharply focussed erudition. M. Koyré is helping the reader or even the rereader to meet Plato face to face for the first time. But there is plenty of internal evidence that he himself has met Plato many times and that his lightest comment is born of a profound textual acquaintance with the philosopher he is writing about. M. Koyré is not writing about *all* the dialogues of Plato, nor does he treat *all* the possible themes. But what he does say is wonderfully suggestive for all else that might be said about Plato. M. Koyré has, in other words, written a little classic about a classic. Fortunately for us, the translation conveys the precise elegance and the disciplined feeling which have gone into the writing itself.

What sort of book about Plato is this? Why another book about Plato where there are already thousands? Well, there are many volumes alledgedly about Plato which are not about that great

Greek writer and thinker at all. They are about orthodoxies that have been offered under his name. They are about systems that have been made about his thought. They are about everything but the dialogues themselves, and often they only confuse rather than help the reader when he comes to reading those. There are books about books about Plato. There are studies by historians of his time or by philologians who debate his grammar, or theologians who fortify themselves with ambiguous Platonic phrases made more ambiguous out of their context. There are A. E. Taylor's patient critical summaries of the dialogues; there is Paul Shorey's attempt to demonstrate the "Unity" of Plato's thought.

In all the literature on the subject there are very few books which start where M. Koyré starts, with the dialogues themselves, and place the reader almost at once where he should be placed, in the situation of a reader of the dialogue, a hearer almost, or what M. Koyré suggestively terms a "reader-auditor." M. Koyré seizes upon the peculiar paradoxes of the dialogues, paradoxes which his analysis makes much less baffling. There is the apparent inconclusiveness of the dialogues in writings which are obviously serious in their moral intentions. I leave it to the reader to see how skilfully M. Koyré enables him to see the senses in which the dialogues are on the surface inconclusive, but the sense, too, in which the central theme of the moral and theoretical supremacy of knowledge is always uttered and reuttered. I leave it to the reader, too, to discover in M. Koyré's pages the subtle philosophical meaning of the dialogue form itself, the texture and the point of the Socratic irony and the Socratic questioning, the force of the allusions to the poets and to the statesmen of the time, the dramatic emphasis of the very quality of the persons making the points made.

The reader will learn above all from M. Koyré how to read the Platonic dialogues. He will do this not by any rigid schoolmaster's

Foreword vii

formula, but by the sensitized perception opened of an imaginative critic. For the fact is that Plato is in a way harder to read than more systematic philosophers. He is more difficult, as M. Koyré points out, because he is an aristocratic artist who will not underline morals and underscore ideas. No summary of one of Plato's dialogues is an account of what dramatically and intellectually each dialogue is. M. Koyré takes some of the most characteristic of the highly dramatic works, notably the *Meno*, the *Protagoras*, the *Charmides*, the characteristically Socratic dialogues, and does not either summarize or expound them. He insinuates the reader with deceptive ease into the living mood and movement of the dialogue itself, and he makes the reader aware almost as the dialogue itself does to the experienced student what Socrates is pictured by Plato as wishing to make his listener feel. At the end of M. Koyré's examination of the *Theaetetus*, for example, one realizes, I think, as one may presume Socrates intended Theaetetus to realize, that he knows the failures of conventional conceptions of knowledge, that he has intimations of at least in what direction knowledge is to be sought. M. Koyré leads the reader skilfully through the steps by which Plato makes his reader-auditor aware of the necessity of the soul ultimately talking to itself with sufficient rationality so that it uncovers within itself the meaning that is knowledge, reality become self-evident to reason.

M. Koyré, without in the least forcing Plato the artist into a system of a presumed Plato the schoolmaster, does indicate the vital recurrence of certain central themes in Plato and the way in which these themes are bound together in the moral unity of life as mastered and understood by reason. He makes clear the union of theory and action, of philosophy and politics. I know of no other place in the critical literature on the subject where the reader will learn better to understand the manner in which education of an *élite*, expert, responsible and disinterested, is conceived and worked out, the way in which education is used to make philosophical understanding available as the guide and reformer of the "imperfect cities" of men.

There are, perhaps, certain themes which M. Koyré leaves untouched, the cosmological considerations raised in the *Timaeus*, the theme of Eros in the *Phaedrus* and the *Symposium*, the latter, perhaps, a little more relevant to Professor Koyré's main theme of the dialectic of knowledge and the supremacy of reason that one might at first guess. But an Introduction cannot be an introduction to everything in Plato, and I think most careful students of Plato would feel that the author of this brief study has provided the keys to understanding every theme in Plato by his analysis of two, the relation of knowledge and virtue, of philosophy and politics. One of the merits of the book is that, although not a dialogue itself, yet it almost reads like one, for it gives the effect of a conversation with a learned student of Plato who is eager to make the novitiate feel what he has felt, understand what he has discovered in his author. M. Koyré does not merely impart information, he suggests overtones and analogies. Thus, he is not afraid to point out resemblances between the tyrant state Plato discusses and tyrant states of our own day. And, though he does not force the note, he gently intimates to the reader the way in which the discovery of one's own intentions through careful dialectic bears resemblances to the techniques of modern psychoanalysis. The manner in which the sicknesses of the soul and the sicknesses of societies as suggested by Plato have modern equivalents in fact and in theoretical understanding becomes also the neat subject of M. Koyré's alert criticism.

The best of many good things to which the reader's attention may be called are the effortless, or apparently effortless, elicitation of the very quality of the Platonic method and of the Platonic temper and the consistency with which M. Koyré is trying to lead the reader to Plato, not away from him into some fine-spun specu-

Foreword

lation of the commentator. The net result is that the reader, new or old, will be tempted to turn to Plato himself. But he will do so having come in his initiation by M. Koyré to feel himself to be in the course of this initiation in the hands of a philosopher, and a truly Platonic one. For an American reader this book will be not only an introduction to Platonic scholarship and Platonic understanding, but a meeting with the very finest kind of clarifying erudition. M. Koyré's work is not the exhaustive and exhausting tome of the Germans or the often rambling essay of the English. It is a concentration of much thought and much scholarship into an instrument of analysis and contagious communication. It is an example of philosophy at its French best. It is an example of Platonic insight and Socratic method as well as an introduction to them.

IRWIN EDMAN

New York
March 19, 1945

Contents

FOREWORD, BY IRWIN EDMAN   V

THE DIALOGUE

PHILOSOPHIC DIALOGUE	1
THE MENO	7
THE PROTAGORAS	17
THE THEAETETUS	33

POLITICS

POLITICS AND PHILOSOPHY	53
THE JUST CITY	71
IMPERFECT CITIES	93
CONCLUSION	106

INDEX   113

The Dialogue

PHILOSOPHIC DIALOGUE

To READ Plato is not only a great pleasure, it is a great joy. So admirable is his unique perfection of form, happily allied with unique profundity of thought, that the texts have resisted relentless time. They have not aged. They remain always alive—as alive today as they were in the far-distant era when they were composed. The somewhat indiscreet and puzzling questions—What is virtue, courage, piety? What do these terms really mean?—questions with which Socrates vexed and exasperated his fellow citizens, are as pertinent, even as embarrassing and as annoying as ever. That is probably why he who reads Plato experiences at times a certain feeling of uneasiness, of perplexity; the same, no doubt, as was experienced by Socrates's contemporaries in days gone by.

The reader would like nothing better than to learn the answers to the problems placed before him by Socrates. But those answers are just what Socrates most often denies him. The dialogues, at least the so-called Socratic dialogues, the only ones which will concern us here,[1] leave us up in the air. The discussion ends upon a note of impotence with an avowal of ignorance. By his insidious and precise questions, by his pitiless and subtle dialectic, Socrates makes short shrift of showing up the weakness of his interlocutor's arguments, the lack of foundation for his opinions, the inanity of his beliefs. But when the latter, at bay, turns against Socrates and asks him in turn, "And thou, Socrates, what dost thou think?" Socrates retreats. It is not his business, he tells us, to emit opinions and formulate theories. His role is only to question others. For his part, all he knows is that he knows nothing.

[1] The dialogues of Plato's youth and maturity are called "Socratic." Socrates plays the central role in them; the problem discussed is most often a moral problem. Generally these dialogues "do not lead to any positive conclusion."

It is readily understandable that the reader does not feel entirely satisfied, that he finds himself engulfed by a vague suspicion, and that he is unmistakably though gropingly under the impression that he is being mocked.

Historians and critics of Plato [2] are usually reassuring. The general structure, as also the peculiarities of the Socratic dialogues, and notably the absence of any conclusions are to be explained, so we are told, by the very fact that they are Socratic, that is to say, by the fact that they reproduce more or less faithfully the teachings of Socrates, his free and unacademic conversations in the streets and palaestrae of Athens. The Platonic dialogue, whether it be composed by Plato, Xenophon, or Aeschines of Sphettus, is not designed to indoctrinate us—a doctrine being something Socrates never possessed, as everyone knows, and as he tells us himself over and over again—but rather to present us with an image, the radiant image of the philosopher condemned to death, to defend and perpetuate his memory, and in so doing to bring us his message.

This message, we are told, is indubitably philosophic. The dialogues teach a lesson, but not a doctrinaire lesson, we are assured, rather a lesson in method. Socrates teaches us the use and the value of precise definitions of the concepts used in discussion and the impossibility of arriving at such definitions without first having recourse to a critical revision of the traditional notions and the popular conceptions conveyed by and incorporated in language. Thus, the apparently negative result of the discussion is of the utmost value. It is, indeed, very important to know that one does not know; that common meanings and common language, while providing the starting point for philosophic reflection, provide only a starting point and that dialectic discussion aims precisely at surpassing and surmounting such groundwork.

[2] I have thought it best not to burden this little book with erudite notes and references. They are of no utility for the general public, and the specialists in the subject will themselves know how to supply them.

All that is doubtless true—in fact, much truer than is usually admitted. Indeed, this much appears certain—first, that preoccupations with method dominate and determine the entire structure of the dialogues, which have remained because of that very fact unequaled models of philosophic teaching;[3] second, that the destructive catharsis to which they proceed constitutes the indispensable condition for personal reflection and for the liberation that takes place when a soul, freed from error and self-forgetfulness, soars up on its own wings toward the heights to which Socrates summons it. To me it appears equally evident that just because the Socratic message is one of life, not alone of doctrine (which explains why Socrates so often grips us in the midst of life's daily tasks), the image, the example, the very existence of Socrates occupies a central position in the dialogues.

And still, the uneasiness persists. For, despite all the explanations furnished him, the modern reader cannot admit any more than could Socrates's contemporaries that the philosopher's protestations of ignorance are anything other than pure and simple irony. Rightly or wrongly, he persists in believing that Socrates should and could well have given positive answers to the questions he himself raises. His refusal to do so irks the reader, who still thinks he is being mocked.

I believe, for my part, that the modern reader is both right and wrong. He is quite right in believing in the ironic character of Socratic ignorance; he is right also in believing Socrates to be in

---

[3] In a certain sense the dialogue is the form *par excellence* for philosophic investigation, because thought itself, at least for Plato, is a "dialogue the soul holds with itself," and because, moreover, in the dialogue philosophic thought, freeing itself from all control of an external authority, frees itself likewise from its individual limitations by submitting to the control of another thought. The dialogue "gets somewhere" when the interlocutor-investigators agree, that is, when Socrates succeeds in making his interlocutor see the truth as he sees it. The dialogue ends in smoke when the interlocutor refuses to make the effort, as in the *Gorgias*, or reveals his incapacity to do so, as in the *Meno*.

possession of a doctrine;[4] he is right, finally, in perceiving that Socrates is poking fun. But he is wrong if he believes that the philosopher is making fun of him. The modern reader is wrong if he forgets that he is the reader of the dialogue, not Socrates's interlocutor. For though Socrates often has his fun at the expense of his interlocutors, Plato never mocks his readers.

The modern reader who reads these pages, for instance, may possibly say that all this is too much for his understanding. Upon my word, it is hardly his fault; dialogues belong to a very special literary genre, and for all too long we have ceased to know how to write or even to read them.

The perfection of form of Plato's work is common knowledge. Everyone knows that Plato was not only a great, a very great philosopher, but also (some even say especially) a great, a very great writer. All his critics, all his historians, unanimously praise his incomparable literary talent, the richness and variety of his language, the beauty of his descriptions, the power of his inventive genius. Everyone realizes that Plato's dialogues are admirable dramatic compositions, wherein the ideas and the men who hold them confront and jostle each other before our very eyes. Everyone reading a Platonic dialogue has the feeling that it could be acted, actually transported onto the stage.[5] However, the fitting conclusions are rarely drawn, although they seem to me important prerequisites toward the understanding of Plato's work. Let us try, then, to formulate them as briefly and as simply as possible.

The dialogues, as we have just said, are dramatic works which could and even should be staged. Needless to say, a drama is not played in the abstract before empty benches. It necessarily presupposes a public to which it is addressed. In other words, the drama —or the comedy—implies a spectator, or more properly an audi-

---

[4] A purely critical Socrates seems to me unlikely. The influence he exerted on a mind such as Plato's would be in that case inexplicable.
[5] This has been done. In Cicero's time the Roman intellectuals had the dialogues acted.

Philosophic Dialogue

tor.[6] That is not all: the spectator-auditor has a part, a very important part, to play in the ensemble of the acting. The drama is not a "spectacle," and the public witnessing it do not, or at least should not, conduct themselves purely as "spectators." They must collaborate with the author, understand his intentions, draw conclusions from the action that unfolds before their eyes; they must capture the meaning and become imbued with it. The more perfect and the more truly "dramatic" the work, the more important and the greater is this collaboration of the auditor or of the public. How sorry, indeed, would be the theatrical piece in which the author should place himself in some way upon the stage, there to comment on and to explain himself.[7] Or, conversely, how pitiful would be the public for which such an explanation, such an authorized commentary, would be necessary.

But again, dialogue, at least true dialogue, like Plato's, dialogue in the literary tradition, not a simple expository artifice such as that of Malebranche or Valéry, is a dramatic piece.[8] Whence it follows that in every dialogue there exists besides the two obvious personages—the two interlocutors who discuss—a third, invisible, but present and quite as important, the reader-auditor. Now Plato's reader-auditor, the public for which his work was written, was a singularly well-informed person, aware of many things which we, unfortunately, do not know and doubtless never shall know; he was also singularly intelligent and penetrating. Hence he understood much better than we the allusions strewn throughout the

---

[6] In the drama of antiquity, to a certain extent this role is played by the chorus.
[7] Hence, it is ridiculous to be on the lookout for the author's mouthpiece in a dramatic work of deep significance, such as Shakespeare's. The author expresses himself in and by the ensemble of the work.
[8] The medieval dialogue between the *magister* and the *discipulus*, as well as the modern one, that of Berkeley and Malebranche, Schelling and Valéry—the list could be prolonged—is not *dramatic*. One of the interlocutors, Philonous or Theophile (the name alone well designates them), serves as the author's mouthpiece. The modern dialogue, except perhaps that of Galileo and Hume, reads like any other book.

dialogues, and he was not deceived as to the value of elements that so often appear to us as subordinate. Thus, he comprehended the importance of the dramatis personae, of the actors who were the protagonists of the work in dialogue form. He knew also how to discover for himself the Socratic or Platonic solution for the problems that the dialogue apparently left unsolved.

Apparently—for from our very simple and in fact banal considerations on the dialogue's structure and meaning, one must conclude, it seems to me, that every dialogue carries with it a conclusion. Certainly not a conclusion formulated by Socrates; but one that the reader-auditor is in duty bound and is in a position to formulate.

I fear that the modern reader may not be entirely satisfied. Why, he may ask, all these complications? If Socrates possessed a doctrine, a doctrine with which Plato was perfectly acquainted, to judge by all the evidence, why does he let us flounder about instead of explaining it clearly and simply? And if one were to object that the absence of an explicit conclusion pertains to the very essence of the dialogue,[9] the answer would doubtless be that no one forced Plato to choose this very special mode of exposition and that he could well have written books like everybody else's and so explained Socratic doctrines that all his readers could understand and even learn them.

Once again, the modern reader is simultaneously right and wrong. He is right in judging that the mode of exposition Plato chose did not render Socratic doctrine readily accessible. On the other hand, he is wrong in thinking that Plato ever wished to so present it. Quite the contrary; for Plato this was not feasible or even desirable.[10]

[9] This is not completely the case. Thus, in the *Republic*, as well as in the *Timaeus*, Plato exposes a positive doctrine.
[10] Platonic philosophical teaching is to a certain extent esoteric. This fact must never be forgotten.

As a matter of fact, for Plato real science, the only kind worthy of the name, is not learned from books, is not imposed upon the soul from without; it is attained, discovered, invented by the soul in solitary travail. The questions formulated by Socrates, that is to say, by the one who knows, stimulate, fecundate, and guide the soul (the celebrated Socratic maieutic consists in just that); the soul itself, however, must furnish the response to the questions.

As for those who are incapable of such effort and therefore do not grasp the meaning implicit in the dialogue, so much the worse for them. Plato, in fact, never asserts that science and, of course, philosophy are accessible to all or that everyone is capable of dealing with these subjects. He always taught the contrary. That is precisely why the difficulty inherent in the dialogue, incompleteness, the need for a personal effort on the part of the reader-auditor, is not a defect in Plato's eyes, but quite the reverse, an advantage, even a great advantage, in this type of exposition. It constitutes a test and allows for differentiation between those who understand and those, doubtless the majority, who do not.

But all of this must appear abstract and abstruse. Let us therefore choose a few examples as illustrations.[11]

THE MENO

EVERYONE is acquainted with the charming little dialogue that is named after its principal protagonist, Meno. I shall briefly recall its contents and main threads.[1] The dramatis personae first of all. They are few in number: aside from Socrates, Meno, a Thessalian mercenary who took part in the expedition of the ten thousand with Xenophon and never returned; Anytus, a rich Athenian bourgeois,

[11] I shall choose three, the *Meno,* the *Protagoras,* and the *Theaetetus.*
[1] I have no intention of furnishing herewith an account of or a commentary on the dialogues chosen as examples. My readers, it is hoped, will do that for themselves by reading or rereading Plato.

future accuser of Socrates; finally, an anonymous slave of Meno's.

The dialogue begins abruptly. Point blank, Meno fires at Socrates the fashionable question so often disputed in the philosophic circles of Athens: Can virtue (ἀρετή) [2] be taught or not? And if not, how does one acquire it? Can it be by exercising it, or if not, whence, then, does it come to us? May it be a gift of nature, or is it different in origin? To this avalanche of questions Socrates, of course, is incapable of furnishing a reply. Even worse, not only does he find it impossible to state whether virtue can or cannot be taught, but (and here is the reason for his difficulty) he does not even know what virtue is and has never met anyone who does.

Meno is rather astonished. How can Socrates assert such things? Has he never met Gorgias? But it is not even necessary to evoke Gorgias. Everybody knows what virtue is. He, Meno, first of all. Everyone knows that there are all sorts of virtues: man's virtue and woman's; that of children and that of old people; of slaves and of free men; and so forth. Each situation and each action has its own virtue.[3]

No doubt, answers Socrates; but virtue itself and in itself? Meno does not understand, and Socrates explains to him at length that in order for all these virtues to be "virtues," it is necessary that they all possess a common essence (εἶδος) of which each is naught but a particular manifestation.

[2] It is well known that ancient "virtue" (ἀρετή) differs from Christian virtue; it is something much more virile and in no sense humble. I wonder whether it would not be better in translating this notion to use some term other than "virtue"; for example, the word "valor," in the sense in which one says "valor and discipline," "a man (or a soldier) of valor."

[3] Meno is right: there are different and even incompatible virtues; the virtue of woman is not that of man any more than the horse's virtue can be identified with the elephant's. If Meno had known how to suck the marrow from his idea, he would have attained Aristotle's concept according to which virtue equals perfection. But Meno is not capable of getting to the bottom of the idea, for he refuses to make the effort.

Meno understands, or believes he understands. Virtue in itself? That is very simple; it is the power of command. His definition is obviously worthless. First of all, the power of command is not a virtue unless one adds that it is the power of commanding justly: the tyrant is not a virtuous being. Next, it is clear that Meno has not defined the essence of virtue, but simply a single form of it. Whereupon Socrates once again gives him a lesson in logic, explaining that the fact that the circle is a figure does not authorize us to state that every figure is a circle and that one must define the figure in other terms and without introducing the notion of the circle into the definition.

Meno once again believes he has grasped the point. A general definition is what Socrates wants. That is no obstacle: virtue is nothing other than "the desire for good things joined with the power of procuring them." The new definition is not worth much more than the previous one. First of all, it contains a useless term. "Desire for good things" is a pleonasm. For that matter, everyone desires good things and nothing else.[4] No one desires bad things, unless, of course, he is in error and considers things good which in fact are not. On the other hand, the definition is insufficient. The "power of procuring" is not a virtue in itself (the thief is not a virtuous man). Consequently one must add: in a just manner. However, justice itself being a virtue, it follows that Meno has defined virtue by one of its particular forms, or as Socrates puts it, the whole by means of a part.

We are now back at the point where Meno—who thought he knew—is obliged to admit with Socrates that he has not the least idea what virtue means. The search must be begun all over again. But Meno, who doubtless would like to end it entirely, retreats behind another question, much disputed at the time, and makes the following objection: How can one search for what is totally un-

[4] That is Socrates's fundamental conviction: nobody desires evil or commits it voluntarily.

known? If one were to find it, how can he know he has found what he was seeking?

The objection is plausible and broad in scope. It actually implies that nothing can be learned. Plato, we must admit, at once accepts it in all seriousness. Let us go even farther: Plato accepts it. His well-known theory of reminiscence explains in this connection that the situation—in effect an impossible one—of searching for what one is totally ignorant of never comes to pass. As a matter of fact, we always seek for what we already know. We try to render conscious our unconscious knowledge; we endeavor to recall to mind a forgotten bit of knowledge.[5]

In the *Meno* Socrates answers the objection by evoking a myth and invoking a fact. The myth of the pre-existence of souls permits us to conceive of knowledge as a reminiscence, and the fact that it is possible to teach a science to someone ignorant of it without actually "teaching" him, but on the contrary having him discover it for himself, demonstrates that knowledge is actually merely remembering.[6]

Socrates now proceeds to prove this by the facts. By dint of asking one of Meno's slaves specific questions, at the same time tracing figures in the sand before him, Socrates has him discover a fundamental geometric proposition. The slave had never studied mathematics, so at first he makes mistakes. However, he ends by furnishing the right answers to Socrates's questions, obvious proof that he knows what he is talking about, doubtless without realizing

---

[5] To use a later term, this knowledge is *innate* in the soul.
[6] Plato's historians have as a general rule taken the myth of pre-existence much too seriously; much more so than Plato himself, who, on the contrary, emphasizes the mythical character of that doctrine and indicates quite distinctly that it solves nothing. Indeed, in every anterior existence the problem of knowledge (or of acquiring knowledge) would come up in exactly the same way as in our present existence. Platonic *anamnesis* brings back to our minds knowledge that our soul has always possessed in its own right.

it. Indeed, Socrates's questions teach him nothing, they serve only to recall things to his consciousness, to awaken in his soul dormant and unconscious knowledge that it already possessed.

We now have the answer to the difficulty broached by Meno. Henceforth, at least in Socrates's opinion, nothing prevents us from resuming the search for the definition, or better, for the essence of virtue. But Meno does not understand things thus. He would like to go right back to his first question, namely, "Is virtue something that can be taught, or is it a gift of nature, and by what means can it be acquired?"

Meno's wish is quite unreasonable, as Socrates loses no time in pointing out, since it amounts to wishing to study the properties of a thing of unknown nature. Hence, the question must be approached less directly, it must be treated *ex hypothesi*, that is to say, we must content ourselves with determining the necessary conditions for the teaching of virtue. The answer, in that case, is very simple: for virtue to be taught, it must be a science,[7] science being the only thing that can be taught.[8]

Or, the other way around, if virtue were a science, it could actually be taught. There would be teachers of virtue as there are of all sciences. As a matter of fact, there are none. At least, Socrates has never met any. That is not merely a personal opinion of his; it is shared by Athenians in general. Anytus, who has just arrived

[7] The Greek term ἐηιστήμη means both "science" and "theoretical knowledge" as opposed to τέχνη, practical knowledge. We keep the translation "science" because it is traditional.
[8] Socrates's affirmation may appear no less surprising to the modern reader than to the philosopher's interlocutor. The modern reader could object that many things which are not "sciences" are taught, to wit, arts, crafts, and so forth, and that one learns to speak, to dance, to make music, and so forth. But to understand Socrates's affirmation, it must be realized that for Plato "to learn" (μανθάνειν) implies "to understand." One does not then "learn" crafts, arts, manners, poetry: one is coached or trained in them, or learns them "by heart,"

and has seated himself, probably next to Meno, is going to confirm this, states Socrates.[9]

Anytus is told the argument: Meno "is desirous of acquiring that talent and that virtue by which one governs well at home and in the city, that one honors his parents, that one knows how to receive fellow citizens and foreigners and to take leave of them like an honest man." In brief, Meno wishes to acquire what the Greeks called "political virtue"; in modern terms, he wishes to become a gentleman. To whom must he turn? Perhaps to those who give themselves for masters of virtue, that is, to some sophist. "Heaven forbid!" ejaculates Anytus. No, especially not to any sophist, for even though he has never, thank Heaven, had anything to do with them, Anytus knows all too well that neither they nor their teachings are worth anything. They are truly a pest and a curse.—Well, then, to whom ought one to turn? Anytus is of the opinion that there is no need to look for a teacher. "One may turn to any honest Athenian citizen, who will teach those norms of virtue that he himself has learned from his predecessors. Praise be to the gods, Athens has never been lacking in honest men." Socrates agrees, but that is not the problem. Are those honest men capable of teaching virtue? Anytus answers in the affirmative. However, none of the great figures of Athenian history, neither Themistocles nor Thucydides nor Aristides nor Pericles, ever knew how to teach virtue to anyone, not even to their own children. No doubt they would have done so had it been feasible. It is therefore reasonable to conclude that the task is impossible and that virtue cannot be taught. Anytus finds no retort. Instead, he gets angry and accuses Socrates of belittling Athens and its statesmen.

[9] Anytus, a rich Athenian bourgeois, a person of considerable importance, well-considered in the city, represents social conformism in all its horror; Meno represents the "emancipated" intellectual. As Socrates sees it, in spite of their violent opposition, fundamentally the two characters are perfectly in accord: they both want the same things. The sophist lacks the inhibitions of the conformist: thus, he reveals the true essence of the latter.

The Meno

Anytus, who was absent at the beginning of the dialogue, did not hear Meno's questions and distinctions. What he says is that virtue, like good manners "taught" to children, is acquired by usage and by the imitation of one's parents and ancestors. Anytus's error is understandable; for him, virtue and tradition, established usages, are one and the same thing. Any criticism of social conformity is in his view a crime, and Socrates is no better than a sophist.[10]

Meno picks up the discussion. If virtue cannot be taught, it is not a science, he agrees willingly. In truth, he has long been of this belief, like his master Gorgias, who has always jeered at those among his colleagues who have promised to teach virtue. "The only thing one ought to attempt is to train orators." Nor is virtue a gift of nature like beauty or strength, Meno agrees. Well, then, what is virtue? We still know nothing about it. Socrates remarks, however, that perhaps not all the possibilities of defining virtue have as yet been exhausted. For example, one could admit that it is "true or right opinion" (ὀρθὴ δόξα), that is, something like a belief or a blind conviction, yet well-founded.

Indeed, for all practical purposes, so far as our acts are concerned, true opinion is the equivalent of knowledge. The only thing which distinguishes the two in practice is the instability of the former so long as it is not enchained by reasoning, in which case it would be transformed into science. But once again, in practice true opinion—so long as one has it—suffices. One may then admit that just because Athenian statesmen have had true opinion, on the one hand, they have been able to govern their city successfully; but on the other hand, precisely because all they possessed was true opinion, not science, they have been incapable of transmitting their virtue to their successors. So that "with regard to science

[10] Anytus is not altogether wrong. When all is said and done, Socratic criticism is still more destructive than that of the sophists, from the point of view of conformity and superstitious tradition. Philosophy is a dangerous thing.

they are in no wise different from prophets and soothsayers; for these also often tell the truth without knowing what they are talking about." "Hence those who possess virtue do so by divine favor, without the intervention of intelligence, and it will always be so, unless perchance a statesman be found who can transmit virtue to others," in which case he would be among his colleagues "like a real man among shadows."

"Thus," concludes Socrates, "virtue seems to us to be, in those in whom it manifests itself, the result of divine favor. What, then, does it consist of, properly speaking? Never shall we know with certainty unless before inquiring how virtue comes to man we begin by inquiring what virtue is in itself." But it is growing late, Socrates must be off, and so he departs, leaving his interlocutors and asking Meno to "cool off" his host Anytus.

The dialogue apparently ends in a checkmate, or even a double check. We do not know any more than we knew at the outset what virtue consists of or whether it can be taught. Socrates has succeeded only in "benumbing" Meno by showing him his ignorance and in infuriating Anytus.

No doubt, but whose fault is it? We who have witnessed the dialogue do not hesitate to recognize that the responsibility for the failure lies, not with Socrates, but solely with Meno. The discussion was engaged and led without any regard for logic, because Meno attacked the problem whether virtue can be taught before knowing what it is in itself. And it is Meno, again, who, having understood nothing of the lesson taught him by Socrates in the incident of the slave, refused to approach the study of the principal problem, thereby sidetracking the discussion.

Meno understood nothing of Socrates's lesson—that is putting it too mildly, nothing of Socrates's lessons, I should have said. Not one lesson, but several lessons were furnished him by Socrates, to no avail. When all is said and done, we are hardly surprised, for we who understand them, understand likewise the reason for Meno's lack of comprehension.

First of all, Meno does not know how to think. He does not know what a definition is nor a vicious circle. It is in vain that Socrates explains it to him, he is incapable of learning it. Thus, he does not notice that Socrates, proposing to identify virtue with "true" or "right" opinion (ὀρθὴ δόξα), makes sport of him (but not of us); how, indeed, could one tell that an opinion is "true," that is, in accord with the truth if one does not possess it, in other words, if one does not have science? We understand it, but Meno does not. "What you say there is most interesting, Socrates," is all he manages to respond. Meno understands nothing, not even the ferocious irony of the comparison between the Athenian statesmen and the soothsayers and of the statement that the virtue of the former is a gift of the gods. When Socrates sets up in contrast to these false statesmen the image of the true statesman, who possesses science,[11] "Well put, Socrates," is his sole comment.

Meno does not know how to think, because he has never learned how. For thinking, that is, real thinking, reasoning correctly in accord with the truth, is precisely what constitutes science; it can be "learned" and "taught" (and we who have passed through the hard school of Plato,[12] we know it better than anyone). Yet Meno, friend and disciple of Gorgias, has not learned correct reasoning, but only persuasive discourse. He is not a philosopher; he is merely a rhetorician. Truth matters little to him. What he seeks is not truth, but success.

Meno does not know how to think, precisely because truth is of

[11] He is the statesman, the philosopher-king of the *Republic* and of the *Statesman*.

[12] The method of the Platonic dialectic is exactly that of science: first the statement of the problem, then the formulation of the hypothesis, next the discussion of its implications and consequences, finally the confrontation with undisputed axioms or facts.

little import to him. For to think, to search for truth, to seek to awaken in the soul the "remembrance" of forgotten knowledge, is a difficult thing; it is a serious matter, entailing effort, persevering effort. And that is why thought presupposes a love, a passion, for truth. Thus, intellectual and moral education go of necessity hand in hand.

To think is a serious matter. But Meno does not take the whole affair seriously. The question he puts before Socrates, to wit, "Can virtue be taught?" and the objection he raises, "How search for what we are ignorant of?" are, we know full well, much disputed and fashionable questions, purely rhetorical on Meno's lips. He does not ask them in order to obtain an answer, but rather to be able to discourse with ease. Hence he is painfully surprised to find himself suddenly "benumbed" and "paralyzed" by Socrates's questions, benumbed and paralyzed and not freed from error, "encouraged," and "propelled" toward the search for truth. The hard and arduous dialectic pursuit of the essence of virtue is repulsive to him. That is why he does not understand the lesson contained in the interrogation of the slave. But a still deeper reason constitutes the final explanation for his failure: the essence of virtue is of no interest to him whatsoever.

Meno and virtue, this very *rapprochement* is comic. Oh yes, everybody knows our Meno, friend and pupil of the sophists, sophist himself upon occasion, speculator, adventurer, soldier of fortune—with it all, a fine fellow, likable and educated. At the same time, nobody is oblivious of the fact that the problem of virtue leaves him entirely cold. What he is looking for is something quite different, namely, the "good things" of life—success, riches, power.

The term "virtue" or "virtuous life" means for Meno, as for Anytus and the common people, possession of all these "good things." Thus, for him "to teach virtue" means to teach a technique which brings us to this desired goal. How could he understand Socrates's lesson? Their thoughts move on entirely different planes.

The lesson, however, is sufficiently clear for us to understand it fully. If Socrates was able to "teach" geometry to Meno's slave, it was because in the latter's soul there lay vestiges, traces, germs of geometric knowledge. These seeds of science innate in the soul, as Descartes was to phrase it two thousand years later, stirred, sprouted, and bore fruit in response to the stimulus of Socrates's questions. But they could develop thus only because the slave, convinced of his ignorance, was willing to make the effort necessary to "recall" "forgotten" truths.

It is the same, exactly the same, with virtue. If Meno had been able to or had wished to make the mental effort demanded of him by Socrates, he would have understood, as we understand, that the ideal statesman, able to transmit and "teach" virtue, is for Socrates a valid ideal and that consequently the reasoning by which Socrates demonstrates that virtue is not science (since it is not taught) is not to be taken too literally. Virtue is not taught, but it can be taught. To use a later phrase, *de non esse ad non posse non valet consequentia*. Besides, is it quite true that there are no masters of virtue and that the latter is not taught? Just what is Socrates's business in life? Is it not clear that all his acts, up to and including the discussion with Meno and Anytus, are merely a means of teaching virtue, or, if you prefer, wisdom, which is nothing other than the science of the good? Meno has not understood the lesson, because in his soul there are no longer any living vestiges of the idea of good. Thus, the dialogue's unformulated conclusion, an answer to Meno's question, stands out in bold relief—yes, virtue can be taught, since it is science, but it cannot be taught to Meno.

THE PROTAGORAS

THE SAME QUESTIONS—"What is virtue?" and "Can it be taught?"—constitute the main subject matter of the *Protagoras,* one of the most beautiful and doubtless the most amusing of Plato's dialogues.[1] But the situation that confronts us therein is not exactly the same as in the *Meno*.[2] While Meno has basically no doctrine and throughout the discussion only asks questions, Protagoras on the other hand has a doctrine to be taken in all seriousness. In this way the discussion here is much more advanced and especially much more explicit than that in the *Meno*. The arguments which are only sketchily treated or even merely indicated in the latter dialogue are developed at length in this one. In addition, to refute the great sophist's very solid and inwardly consistent doctrine, Socrates finds himself obliged to put forth and expound one of his own. However, the dialogue ends with the conclusion that Socrates himself qualifies as extremely paradoxical and deceptive. In effect, "Socrates, who denied that virtue can be taught, affirms that it is science, that justice, temperance, and courage is all science, which is the surest means of showing that one can teach virtue; while Protagoras, who had first affirmed as a fact that it could be taught, ends by saying that it is anything but science, which deprives it of any possibility of being taught."

But let us not get ahead of ourselves. Glance through the dialogue—from the literary point of view, a sheer masterpiece. The characters of the drama, or more exactly of the comedy, are numerous and diversified, each acting out his own part, each living his own life, each speaking his own language (Plato is a master of the parody, of writing "in the manner of"). The form Plato adopts, that of a dialogue narrated by Socrates, permits the latter to exercise all his verve at the expense of his adversaries. All is fair in war—irony and joking are two of the polemist's most powerful weapons, ruining the prestige of the party attacked.

[1] The *Protagoras* is as amusing as a comedy of Aristophanes.
[2] I shall not give a full account of the *Protagoras* any more than of the *Meno* or the *Theaetetus*. Thus, I shall pass in silence over the eminently comical scene of the "presentation" of the sophists, in the home of the rich snob Callias, to all the smart set of Athens, the speeches of Hippias and Prodicus, even Socrates's speeches. I refer the reader directly to Plato's text.

The Protagoras

The dialogue starts out with an extremely interesting introduction. Socrates tells how, long before sunrise, he was awakened by his young friend Hippocrates, who the night before had learned of the arrival in Athens of the sophists and without losing a minute had come to ask Socrates to recommend him to Protagoras: "Let us meet with him," he says, "before he goes out. He lives with Callias, the son of Hipponicus. Come, let's be off."

Hippocrates is charming in his youthful ardor, his desire for learning, his enthusiasm for the new wisdom preached by the sophists. Hippocrates! What a pity that we know practically nothing about him. The *Protagoras* was written especially for him, that is, for youths like him. He represents Athenian youth no longer satisfied with the old traditional disciplines, in search of things new—of new values, a new training, a new civilization.

Hippocrates seeks out what is new, without, however, being fully aware of what he wants. That is why one must not be too astonished to hear him ask Socrates to recommend him to the sophists. Plato's auditor-readers have no doubt tasted the irony of the situation. It is clear that Hippocrates, like the average Athenian, is far from knowing how to differentiate between Socratism and Sophistics. They appear to him to be very closely allied. Are they not both opposed to traditional ethics? Do they not both criticize common sense? Do they not both appeal to novelty? That is the reason Socrates agrees to lead him to Protagoras, precisely to confront him with the two doctrines, to permit him to choose between them. The dialogue could have, or should have, been named "Hippocrates at the Crossroads."

The introductory conversation between Hippocrates and Socrates is therefore of capital interest. "What dost thou desire in the main?" Socrates asks his young friend. "What dost thou wish Protagoras to teach thee?" We learn that Hippocrates does not seek to learn a trade or to become a sophist himself; he wants to profit by Protagoras's teachings, to develop his own culture, "in a way befitting a free man," just as he receives the teachings of the grammatist, the zitherist, and the trainer. Very well, but what does this teaching consist of? What art will Protagoras teach him? The art of speaking well, Hippocrates answers. "Speaking well about what?" replies Socrates; "He speaks well who knows what he is talking about." "Just what is this thing that the sophist himself knows and that he makes known to his disciple?" [3]

Hippocrates is perplexed. He does not know what branch of knowledge is the special property of the sophist. The modern reader is equally perplexed, but for a very different reason. He cannot admit that Socrates ignores the existence of rhetoric, "the art of speaking," that he ignores the fact that one learns to speak as one learns to run, to wrestle, or to engage in gymnastics. Consequently, Socrates's questions appear quite sophistical to him. Wrongly so, however. For Socrates does not ignore the existence of rhetoric, he denies its value. Rhetoric for him is not an art, or at least it is a completely inferior art, to be compared, not with fencing or gymnastics, but at best with the art of cooking. With good reason, for the gymnasium teacher who trains and exercises the body knows what is good for it and what is not. But the teacher of rhetoric, although he lays claim to being able to form his disciples' souls, does not know what is good for the soul. If he did, he would be, not a rhetorician, but a philosopher. And there is no use in his telling us that rhetoric is a purely formal art. A purely formal art of speaking would lead to speech without thought, since there is no purely formal thought, as the *Charmides* points out.[4] Hence such an art would not form, but deform the soul unhappily left to its mercy.

Socrates explains to his young friend how imprudent he is to wish thus to entrust his soul, his most precious possession, to some-

---

[3] The Socratic view of eloquence was to be Descartes's and Boileau's.
[4] The philosophical importance of the *Charmides* has been unfortunately almost always unrecognized by the critics.

one he does not even know and whom he calls a "sophist" without even knowing the meaning of the term; to entrust to him his soul, for him to care for, shape, and nourish—for what is science if not the nourishment of the soul?—without knowing whether he will nourish it well or badly, without even knowing whether he knows, as the physician and the trainer do in the case of the body, what is proper and what is improper nourishment for the soul. Is it not prudent to find out these things before acting?

Science, nourishment for the soul—the image is an illuminating one and leads us to understand Socrates's radical opposition to rhetoric, which dresses up what is weak in order that it shall appear strong.[5] In brief, it is the art of producing illusion. Yet not with illusion, but with truth should one nourish one's soul [6] if one wishes to conserve, or to grant it, strength and health.[7]

But let us go on. We shall ask Protagoras himself what he teaches and how we may profit by it. Protagoras, addressing Hippocrates, will answer: "Young man, if thou comest to me, this is what thou wilst profit: after a day spent with me, thou wilst return home a better man, and thus each of thy days will be marked by progress toward perfection." Too vague, in Socrates's judgment; doubtless Hippocrates will grow better and better every day, but at what? And Protagoras answers: "The objective of my teaching is prudence for each man in the ordering of his own household, and as for public affairs, the talent for conducting them to perfection through word and deed." Thus, good citizens and good statesmen are what the sophist claims to shape.

Exactly the objective, it must be pointed out, of "Hippocrates, son of Apollodorus, issue of an illustrious and opulent family . . .

---

[5] The rhetoricians boast of being able to make a weak cause or argument appear strong.

[6] The truth—food for the soul. For Descartes, again, the aim of mathematics is to "feed the soul on truth."

[7] The strength and health of the soul spring from virtue, or, *vice versa*, virtue is health and strength of the soul.

who . . . desires to make a name for himself in the city." Just what Meno, too, was after; it is what the Greeks call virtue, or more exactly "political virtue." Protagoras, we see, offers what is in demand. His ideal is that of the common people; he is no better than they and he offers them no opposition.

But to go on; Protagoras makes pretensions to teaching "political virtue," the implication being that he is a master of that science.[8] But can virtue, political virtue or virtue in general, be taught? Socrates doubts it and counters with an argument that we have already seen utilized in the *Meno*, that the Athenians, who are, however, an intelligent people, do not admit of and do not believe in the existence of experts in this matter. That is why they listen to anybody in matters of state, whereas for technical problems, such as the construction of buildings or ships, they have recourse to the judgment of specialists. Truth to tell, the wisest and the most expert Athenians obviously share this popular view, for they furnish no professors of virtue to their children, nor do they themselves teach them the subject (for instance, in the case of Pericles); it must be that they deem that it is impossible to teach it.

Socrates's argument seems purely ironic to those of us who know his convictions and who know that he is no admirer of Athenian statesmen. But it is valid against Protagoras, who in his conception of virtue does not rise one whit above the popular level, that of Anytus's "average man." Hence Protagoras's answer is the one Anytus indicated without knowing how to develop it.

Virtue, in Protagoras's estimation, not only is taught but also is taught all too frequently. We learn it all our lives; everybody teaches it to us—our parents, our masters, and our fellow citizens. For all members of the city-state possess virtue, justice, and con-

[8] Protagoras claims to be able to teach what we may call "social science," or "science of government." If it were true, we may add in passing, this would make him superior to the great men of the past, who never knew how to transmit their science, or art, to their successors. In this case, Protagoras would be the genuine statesman whose image we glimpsed through the pages of the *Meno*.

science, necessary conditions for the very existence of the city; all, then, teach these things to each other mutually. That is just why specialists in virtue are commonly deemed unnecessary. Thus, contrariwise to what Socrates claims, we all believe that virtue can be taught. We see this from the fact that we blame and reprimand those who are wanting in it. As a matter of fact, are not blame and reprimand forms of lesson?

If, then, virtue is the prerogative of all members of the city, one will understand why the children of great statesmen are not privileged in comparison with those of other citizens. Virtue being taught by everybody to everybody, the teaching is the same for all. Consequently natural gifts in this direction—although virtue is not purely and simply a gift of nature—make themselves felt. Similarly, if everybody learned and taught music, the children of great musicians would not necessarily be very good musicians themselves.

Virtue, then, is learned, like a mother tongue that no one teaches to children because everyone does. It is none the less true that some people are particularly apt at such teaching, and that is the claim Protagoras asserts for himself.[9]

Protagoras's thesis—a very forceful one, as I have already stated—is that of a consistent and conscious social relativism.[10] He has no intention of making innovations or of reforming society or its conception of "virtue." What he promises—and his success

[9] If he had lived at a somewhat later date, Protagoras would have been able to say: everyone teaches children their mother tongue, but I am a grammarian.
[10] The modern reader has no doubt frequently a tendency to feel himself in agreement with Protagoras. That is because the modern reader is so often as much infected with sociologic relativism as Protagoras himself and is no better than he at distinguishing manners from morals. Beyond doubt Protagoras's sociologic relativism, like that of the "philosophy of enlightenment," to which sophistry has sometimes been compared, played an eminently important role in the destruction of the "prejudices," the "biases," the "idols" of Greek thought (and of modern thought). Sociologic relativism is eminently reasonable and becomes an error only when it sets itself forth as absolute.

proves that he keeps his promise—is to analyse in its structure, the mores (νόμος) of a given society or to teach us how to conform to it, how to obtain the approbation of the members of the community in question, how to attain riches, influence, power. But he cannot teach us what aim we have to follow, except to tell us that there again we must conform to the wishes of the community, and thus, in fact, abandon all those claims to supreme knowledge which, according to Socrates and even Protagoras, characterize the statesman.

But there is something else; Protagoras's social relativism obliges him to accept at face value popular notions concerning virtue. Now, these conceptions, like all common-sense notions, are incoherent, confused, and even contradictory,[11] as Socrates is going to show us. Both the average man and Protagoras speak of virtue, justice, wisdom, courage, and so forth. But what are these? Neither Protagoras nor the common people know, for the very reason that they do not know how to find out. Constricted by the forms of language, they cannot go on to grasp the meaning of the objects themselves, or better, the essences which words designate, however vaguely and imperfectly; hence, they do not understand that different virtues partake of one and the same essence, namely, science, or knowledge. One virtue implies the other, and all of them are thus intermingled, even courage, which is knowledge of what is to be feared, and what is not, in other words, of what is "truly terrible." In modern terms, virtue implies a scale of values and is naught but the knowledge of this scale; virtuous conduct necessarily results from knowledge of the good, since for Socrates, as for Spinoza, to know, to judge, and to act are all one.

[11] Protagoras doubtless knows that popular conceptions are incoherent and valueless; and his relativism, which places the manners and customs, the mores of different societies on the same level, plays a critical and destructive role with respect to such notions, exactly analogous to the role played by Montaigne's skepticism, or the social relativism of our day. Thus, like the followers of this modern trend, he is "progressive," and "liberal."

But let us return to the dialogue. Protagoras, we have just seen, is of the opinion that virtue can be taught. How could he possibly doubt it, when he makes a profession of teaching it? He, too, like Meno, without any preliminary definition of the term "virtue," has launched forth into a discussion of the question—Can virtue be taught, or not? As a matter of fact, no more than Meno is he capable of furnishing any response to Socrates's question: "What is virtue?" or, in other words, "Is virtue a unique whole, of which justice, prudence, and saintliness (δικαιοσύνη καὶ σωφοσύνη καὶ ὁσιότης) are parts, or are the aforesaid virtues simply different names for a single whole?"

Let us understand clearly: Socrates's question implies the problem of the unity or the sameness of the different, or, more properly, of the unity of the species of one genus, or, better yet, the problem of the unity of the particularizations of one essence (εἶδος). Protagoras is incapable of answering the question for the simple reason that he does not understand it. But on the other hand, just because he does not understand it, he deludes himself into thinking he is equipped to tackle it: "Nothing easier . . . virtue is one entity . . . and virtues . . . are its component parts." The relationship between the whole and its parts is far from simple; it is in fact extremely difficult to determine with exactitude. Hence Socrates seeks to pin Protagoras down to something precise by offering him a choice between two cases where this relationship appears to be present in material things: "Is it the way parts of the face—the mouth, the nose, the eyes, the ears—form part of the face, or the way parts of a piece of gold that in no wise differ from each other, or each particle from the whole, except for the dimensions?" Although Protagoras has affirmed that virtue is one, he cannot get himself to choose the second part of the alternative. He admits, with the common man, that virtues have something in common, but that nonetheless they differ from each other. Are we not aware that the virtues do not fall by lot all to the same man, "for many individuals are just without being wise, or brave without being just"? Consequently he decides upon the first part of the alternative: the virtues are with respect to each other and to the whole, in the same relationship as the parts of the face.

Now if this were so, if the virtues formed each a separate and self-determinate entity, "having each its particular property," if they differed among themselves as eyes differ from ears, if, in other words (to use terms that doubtless are not Plato's, but which enable us the better to grasp the problem in question), the virtues formed only a mechanical or even an organic whole, it would immediately follow therefrom that they do not possess any internal connection, or natural identity and that, contrary to Protagoras's first affirmation, virtue would not be one, but many. It would have to be said then that no "part" of virtue resembles any other part and that between science ($ἐπιστήμη$), justice, saintliness, prudence ($σωφροσύνη$), and courage ($ἀνδρεία$), there is nothing in common. But let us pursue the analysis. "Together let us try to discover the proper nature of each of them. First of all, is justice a certain thing ($πρᾶγμα$) or is it nothing?" For if it is "a thing," that is, a reality, as Protagoras willingly admits, and if the same is true of saintliness, wisdom, courage, in other words, if the terms by which we designate the virtues are not five different names for a single entity, but, on the contrary, correspond each one to a distinct reality, to an object having its own character, such that it cannot be identified with another, a man may wonder whether this "thing," this "object," this entity that we call "justice" (or saintliness) is in itself a just or an unjust thing (saintly or not). If with everybody else we refuse to admit that justice can be something unjust or that saintliness can be something that is not saintly—"what would be it if saintliness were not it?"—it would necessarily result "that saintliness is a thing the nature of which is not to be just, and justice a thing the nature of which is not to be saintly, as likewise saintliness is non-just and therefore without justice, while justice is without saintliness." The conclusion is one that neither Socrates, who judges, on the contrary, that saintliness is just and that justice is saintly, nor Protagoras himself would be willing to accept.

It is probable that the modern reader will find Socrates's reasoning rather verbalistic and even flavored with sophistry. He will no doubt consider with Protagoras that Socrates is certainly going a bit too far; that by so reducing all relationships between objects to identity and absolute difference (which is the common trick of sophists), one may demonstrate anything one cares to; and he will judge that Protagoras is correct in objecting that "those parts of the face the properties of which we were distinguishing between a little while ago and that we deemed dissimilar, are not, however, lacking in internal resemblances, nor are they without some rapport" and that in consequence nothing prevents us from admitting analogous resemblances and relationships between different kinds or "parts" of virtue.

On the other hand, it is probable that Plato's reader-auditor had a quite different attitude, even a diametrically opposed attitude, to the effect that Socrates's reasoning was perfectly correct and that given the contradictory and untenable premises admitted and accepted by Protagoras, one could not end up with different conclusions. Would not Protagoras have recognized this himself, if he had cared to make the necessary effort and put his thoughts in order?

Indeed, Protagoras admitted that virtues are "things," real objects, not names that cover up or express the concepts, the beliefs, and the conventions of society. Having admitted it, as a sensualist who knows no other reality than that which is accorded the senses, he could not help but accept material objects such as gold and the face as exemplifying the structure of those "realities" and possible relationships that they can maintain among themselves. Thus, for example, he admitted that those realities, or "things"—justice, saintliness—possess a character of their own, a nature ($δύναμις$) which makes them the way they are, or rather what they are. If it be true that gold or any other material object possesses such a "nature"—is it not clear, at least for those of us who, thanks to Socrates (or Plato), know that these "natures" or characters are not material objects, but something quite different from them—is it not clear, then, that those "natures" themselves have not and can never have "natures" that would make them what they are? And why be astonished if Protagoras, committing this elementary error of admitting that justice is not "justice" but just, as if it were a man or an action, be led to separate these "natures" as rigidly as if they were objects or material things?

Indeed, if Protagoras refuses to admit the inevitable consequences and, instead, goes back to the common-sense viewpoint, is that not an indication that for him the discussion is not serious, that the nature of virtue makes very little difference to him, and that the sole factor of interest so far as he is concerned is to show off his, Protagoras's, own skill and his capacity for teaching "political virtue," whatever be its relationship with the other virtues? Is that not the reason why every time the discussion rises above the level of popular conceptions he loses interest and leaves to Socrates the responsibility of carrying out the analysis, punctuating it with a polite, though bored, "if you wish" here and there and showing no real interest until, pressed by Socrates's pitiless questions, he sees himself doomed to defeat? His prestige and reputation are far more important to him than the unity or multiplicity of virtue. With bad grace and only to avoid admitting his own inferiority in the discussion, Protagoras finally picks up the conversation where he left off, but only after having instituted with Socrates an oratorical contest the subject of which was a commentary on a poetical passage, which affords him the opportunity to pronounce a fine speech that Socrates answers in a counter speech of finished irony and dazzling verve.[12]

---

[12] Literary criticism, interpretation of classical poets, was one of the main bases of the teaching given by sophists. The instruction is given in lectures,

The Protagoras

The attempt to determine the connections between virtue and the virtues was a failure. And we are all aware why: because the attempt was made to determine those analogies—and to resolve the question "Can virtue be taught or not?"—without first (as ought to have been done) trying to define virtue. We understand this full well. Unfortunately, Protagoras did not grasp Socrates's lesson. Hence he merely modifies slightly his response. He no longer claims that the virtues all differ from one another, at least in an absolute sense. No, resemblances, similarities, and affinities link them together, at least some of them, such as wisdom, prudence, saintliness, and justice. As for courage, that remains quite another matter. Where courage is concerned, Protagoras maintains his thesis, in line with common sense: courage has nothing to do with other kinds of virtue.

As a matter of fact, despite the airs of superiority that Protagoras assumes when he makes a show of mistrusting common sense and popular opinions (Socrates does not really scorn them, but strives to throw light upon them by revealing their underlying *raison d'être*), it is not only with respect to courage that he firmly holds to the common-sense level. Does he not admit with the mass of men that injustice can be "good," that is, advantageous and profitable to the one who commits it? Does he not accept the popular belief that the good exerts little attraction over human nature, that consequently man does not willingly pursue it, and that that is why, although he knows good, he rarely follows the road that his knowl-

---

because the aim of the education is oratory. Socrates's lecture, in which by dint of the most far-fetched interpretations he accomplishes the startling *tour de force* of enlisting the testimony of the poets in favor of his moral thesis—nobody commits evil voluntarily—serves to contrast the method of the step by step dialectic analysis by question and answer used throughout the dialogue, with Protagoras's rhetorical method. It also shows us the fallacious character of the appeal to the authority of the poets or sages whose lifeless texts are susceptible of the most diversified interpretations or misinterpretations, that they must perforce submit to passively without the power of response and protest.

edge points out, but turns astray from it, "vanquished," as he puts it, by passion or pleasure?

Doubtless Protagoras claims to reject the popular belief that knowledge is a feeble thing of no consequence. He is in agreement with Socrates, he states, in maintaining that knowledge is something very powerful and that wisdom and science constitute the greatest of human forces. But in point of fact he has no more understanding than the common man of the role of knowledge in the structure of our motivation and actions. Perhaps because he knows not what it is.

Thus, he does not realize that man always and everywhere, seeks the good—his good, what is good, useful, and agreeable for him—and flees evil, or what is harmful to him and makes him suffer. He does not realize that nobody acts otherwise and that it is reasonable and well to act thus. Therefore, to feel attracted toward pleasure is no sign of weakness, nor is it in any way to be construed as misconduct, since it is evident that pleasure is a good and pain an evil.

Protagoras objects, "But are not some pleasures bad and some pains good, some agreeable things not good and some disagreeable things not bad?" To which Socrates retorts, "Not at all. Insofar as they are agreeable, they are good; insofar as they are disagreeable, they are bad." Doubtless the criterion is whether they produce disagreeable or agreeable consequences. So, for example, the pleasures that bring on sickness or ruin and the pains that we suffer from curative medicines may be considered "bad" or "good." The price of pleasures may be too high, but that is a matter for calculation. In such calculation, we may make mistakes, all the more readily in that we are unacquainted with the rules, the right way to measure and to evaluate comparatively the different kinds of pleasures and pains, and we do not take into account the effects of temporal perspective which, just as spatial perspective makes far-off objects appear smaller and nearer objects larger, makes future pleasures and pains appear less important and weaker than those we experience in the present.[13]

Socrates goes on to outline the idea, so typical of Bentham, of a sort of mathematical axiology, an art or science to measure moral phenomena or values. "We shall perceive later just what science and what art are involved," he tells us. We immediately perceive that it is not pleasure or anything of the sort that gets the better of us and gains the upper hand over the science of good, but that bad conduct, that is, the wrong choice between good and evil, is a result of ignorance, of lack of knowledge, in other words, the effect of "lying and false opinions about things of value."

Of these "lying and false opinions" the hedonism, which sees value only in bodily pleasure and ignores the higher values of the soul, is, of course, an example. The common morality, which sees value in the good things of life and is just as blind to these higher values, is another.

Lying and false opinions, lack of knowledge—we well understand the error of the popular conception, that conception shared by Protagoras, according to which we can "know good and commit evil." We understand that this conception is founded on ignorance of true value and of true knowledge. We are well aware that despite Protagoras's denials, he deems knowledge a weak thing, inasmuch as he has no realization that knowledge is only the "presence in the soul of the very thing that is known or understood"; he does not

[13] It may seem strange to see Socrates defend against Protagoras the hedonistic thesis of the value of pleasure, and the temptation is great to explain this seeming inconsistency by admitting that Socrates expresses not his own view, but that of the mass, the common people, the οἱ πολλοί, in order to show that even from this point of view it is not passion, but knowledge or ignorance that determines our conduct. I do not believe this explanation to be true. It is not Socrates, but Protagoras who represents the inconsistent morals of the οἱ πολλοί. Socrates is obviously not a hedonist. But the hedonist does not err in recognizing the value of pleasure. He errs in not recognizing the existence of other and higher values.

know in what respect knowledge, that is, possession of the truth, differs from opinion.

We are now in a position to approach the problem of courage and that of cowardice. We see that there, too, it is a question of knowledge, balance, and evaluation. The popular concept, according to which the brave man seeks out danger and the cowardly man runs away from it, is erroneous. Nobody but the fool seeks danger as such, since everybody fears what is harmful and seeks to avoid it, or at least, if that is not possible, to choose the lesser of two evils. The difference, then, between the coward and the brave man is that the former is mistaken as to the nature of the evil that he must avoid at any cost, and the value he has to preserve. He believes that it is his life that he has to preserve and his death that he has to avoid. He does not know that there are evils much worse than loss of life. The brave man knows it; he knows that there are values much higher than life. Thus illuminated and fortified by knowledge, he marches off to battle with a firm step.

Protagoras bows before defeat. Socrates has come out of the tourney victorious. Protagoras is a good sport and will not dispute the palms. But just where have we gotten at the end of it all? At first glance, at least, nowhere. We have arrived at the conclusion that all virtue is knowledge, science of the good. It ought therefore to be teachable, for, as we all admit, what is science can be taught, and what can be taught is science. Yet, as we already know, Socrates, who affirms that virtue is science, denies that it can be taught; and Protagoras, who claims to teach it, does not admit that virtue is science. But the reader-auditor well realizes that contradiction and paradox are only apparent: for if virtue is what Protagoras thinks it is, virtue is certainly not science and Socrates is right in asserting that it can not possibly be "taught." On the other hand, if virtue is what Socrates thinks it is, that is, an intellectual and hence intuitive science of values and the good, then virtue can be "taught." Obviously Protagoras is not the man to do it. Who is? The answer is clear—Socrates. In other words, the philosopher; for the science that Socrates promised to reveal to us at a later date, the science of measure of values, is none other than, as we already know, philosophy.[14]

THE THEAETETUS

The *Theaetetus*,[1] which may be considered the last of Plato's Socratic dialogues, does not afford us the wealth of drama found in the *Protagoras*. The number of interlocutors is very small—Socrates, Theodorus, Theaetetus. The close-knit, technical discussion very often degenerates into a monologue. However, that is readily understandable; the problem dealt with, the nature of science, would lend itself with difficulty to any other treatment.

Nevertheless, the literary structure of the *Theaetetus* presents a curious particularity, upon which it would be well to dwell a moment. The *Theaetetus* is actually a dialogue that was read, or more exactly, written and read. The introduction, a preliminary conversation between two of Socrates's former companions, Terpsion and Euclid,[2] reveals to us the *occasionem legendi:* Euclid has just met Theaetetus, who is being brought back to Athens from camp in Corinth. Theaetetus, wounded and sick, is going home to die. And Euclid, at the thought of the irreparable loss entailed by the death of such a man, "marvels at how characteristically pro-

[14] Virtue cannot be "taught from outside" (διδάσκειν) any more than any true science, but only discovered by ourselves in our own soul. Science is intuitive knowledge that nobody can instill in us; therefore, what Protagoras is "teaching" his pupils cannot be "science," and, consequently, cannot be virtue.

[1] Let me repeat once again, I am not engaged in doing an account of or a commentary on the *Theaetetus*. Hence I shall not mention Socrates's conversation with Theodorus or his speech on the philosopher, which in other respects are extremely important.

[2] Both of them were present at the deathbed of Socrates. Euclid, of Megara, was a follower of Parmenides, the founder of the Megaric school of philosophy. We know nothing about Terpsion.

phetic were Socrates's words about him. Shortly before his death, he met Theaetetus, still an adolescent; seeing him at close range and conversing with him, he felt a keen admiration for his fortunate disposition . . . and told me that he would become famous without fail if he reached the age of manhood." This conversation with Theaetetus was related by Socrates to Euclid, who wrote it down, but in the form of direct dialogue "in order to avoid the awkwardness produced by such interlocutory necessities as 'I said,' 'he agreed,' etc." This is the manuscript that Euclid orders a slave to bring out and read.

The foremost critics of the *Theaetetus* are generally of the opinion that the reasons proffered by Euclid are simply the exposition by Plato himself of the motives for which henceforth he is to abandon the narrative style of the great dialogues of his maturity and return to the simpler manner of his youth. They add that the far more technical character of his later works is better presented, as I have said, by this more direct literary composition. The introduction, then, was designed to furnish us this explanation and at the same time to glorify the great departed scientist, to recall the probably historic fact of his meeting with Socrates, to bring into relief once again the perspicacity of the latter and his benefactory influence upon youth; finally, by having Euclid write down the dialogue, to render indirect homage to this old comrade of many a past contest.

All that is quite likely. We could even add that by letting Euclid write out the dialogue Plato gives us a hint of the fictitious, nonhistoric character of its contents; that at the same time, by this homage to his old friend and opponent, in spite of the criticism of the Megaric eristic to be found in the dialogue, Plato gives us to understand that this criticism is not directed against Euclid, nor against his master Parmenides. Yet all that does not explain why Euclid and Terpsion have the dialogue in question read to them. It is possible, of course, that there is no real problem there and that

The Theaetetus

Terpsion and Euclid act thus because no one acted otherwise—in other words, because nobody read the dialogues as books, at least as we read books—and everybody had them read out loud.[3] That is possible, and it would be interesting in itself.[4] But perhaps it is a question of something else, namely, a very precise reminder of what goes without saying, but is still better said, that the dialogue is written for auditors, in fact for very superior auditors like Theaetetus's two friends, well up on Socratic doctrines and philosophy in general. In that case Plato would be addressing a warning to us by telling us in his way: Beware! this dialogue is not for beginners; it takes up difficult matters; if you wish to understand, put yourself in the place of Terpsion or Euclid; do not forget that they are there.

The characters of the dialogue are well known to us—Theodorus of Cyrene, a good mathematician, a good astronomer, a good professor—and Theaetetus, Plato's companion, teaching member of the Academy, one of the leading geometers of his time. Ideal interlocutors for a scientific discussion. And yet the dialogue ends with an avowal of ignorance and an appeal to future research—a negativistic conclusion, as always, and as always of major importance, at least for us auditors. We observe throughout, and the observation still holds today, that science and philosophy are two separate things; that one may be an excellent scientist without having the least idea of what one is really doing. It is even almost always thus.[5]

The dialogue begins with the introductory description of young Theaetetus. Socrates, eternally on the lookout for young men of promise, asks Theodorus whether among his pupils there is any young man worthy of mention. And Theodorus praises Theaetetus's

[3] In ancient times reading aloud had more significance than we can possibly imagine.
[4] Let us recall in passing that "to read" is rendered in Greek by ἀναγιγνώσκειν, which means, literally, to recognize and to recite by heart.
[5] Books of "scientific philosophy" written by the most celebrated modern scientists confirm Plato's opinion.

marvelous nature. Intellectual gifts beyond compare, which are rarely found together in one person—rapid comprehension and perfect memory—accompanied by equally rare moral qualities—sweetness, modesty, courage—the whole constitutes a unique ensemble. Alas, his external appearance is not on the same plane; he resembles Socrates, yes, he is snub-nosed and as ugly as the great teacher. We savor the joke, and we understand that Theaetetus also is gifted philosophically—has a "philosophical nature," which Theodorus, not being a philosopher, cannot see; Socrates, on the other hand, will take it in at first glance.

They engage in conversation, and Socrates, after stating that he has always believed that science and wisdom are one and the same—a natural remark in a learned milieu—admits that he is not so clear about what science really is. Can Theaetetus inform him? The latter judges that it is very simple to do so: everything one learns from Theodorus, geometry, astronomy, etc.; also techniques and arts—all that is science ($\dot{\epsilon}\pi\iota\sigma\tau\eta\mu\eta$).

We see the point clearly; like Meno, Theaetetus misunderstands Socrates's question (which happens often in the Socratic dialogues), and instead of a definition, he offers us a collection of examples. But unlike Meno, when Socrates makes him see the fallacy he commits, he understands perfectly. The problem put before him by Socrates says he is exactly of the same type as the one he has just solved, to wit, to furnish a general definition of irrational "numbers," a definition obtained by means of a double dichotomy, first dividing all the numbers into "squares" and "oblongs" and calling the equal factors of the square numbers "lengths" ($\mu\hat{\eta}\kappa o s$). As for the oblong numbers, we first transform them into squares, and the equal sides of the squares thereby arrived at we call "powers" ($\delta\acute{v}\nu\alpha\mu\iota s$). Thus the oblong numbers have in a sense equal factors. The whole series of numbers will therefore be represented by a series of squares, and their roots (incommensurable by themselves, but giving rise to a commensurable series) by a series of "lengths"

The Theaetetus

and "powers." [6] Socrates is delighted, and to tell the truth, with good reason. He thereupon encourages Theaetetus: "Take as a model your response to the question on powers and, just as you were able to include their plurality under the unity of their apparent form, strive to make a single definition applicable to the plurality of sciences." The young man hesitates, however; the problem preoccupies him, but he does not see his way through it, and Socrates, to embolden him, explains that the confusion and the pangs that he feels are just the indication that his soul is laboring with thought. He, Socrates, the son of a midwife, has inherited her art in a sense; with this difference, however—he attends not women, but men, and delivers not bodies, but souls. Like the midwives, then, he himself is barren,[7] but he has great skill in aiding young men to give birth to their ideas and in discerning whether the fruit of their efforts is healthy and robust or, on the contrary, weak and badly formed. The operation is all the more necessary and all the more difficult in that the mind, unlike the body, is sometimes delivered not of a real offspring, but merely of an empty shadow. Hence he offers his art for the benefit of Theaetetus: "tackle the question again, Theaetetus; try to tell what constitutes science." And the young man, encouraged and subjugated by Socrates, answers: "In my opinion, at least in my present opinion, science is nothing other than sensation." "Not a banal opinion," answers Socrates, who adds "that is the very opinion of Protagoras. His formula is a bit different, but it amounts to the same thing. He affirms approximately the following: man is the measure of all things; for those which are, the measure of their being; for those which are not, the measure of their nonbeing. You've probably read

---

[6] The reader will find any further information desired on this problem in M. A. Dies's introduction to his edition of the *Theaetetus* (Collection Guillaume Budé, Paris, 1924).

[7] Only a woman who can no longer bear children can be a midwife; even then, only if in her time she has had children of her own. Socrates thus gives us to understand that he, too, has begotten "children."

that somewhere?" "Yes," avows Theaetetus; "in fact very frequently."

Theaetetus's sensationalism thus implies Protagorean relativism. The two are even identical, and the relativism of Protagoras in turn, as Socrates explains to us at length, necessarily implies a metaphysics of flux in the Heraclitean manner. This doctrine of flux leads in the last resort to the conception of a world where nothing is, where nothing lasts more than an instant, where everything flows, locally and qualitatively, that is, changes place and determination at every instant. In such a world of pure multiplicity, where no unity is to be found, there will obviously never be object or subject, and no assertion and hence no science will ever therein be possible. Thus it is that absolute sensationalism destroys itself.[8]

Let me remind the reader that I have no intention of furnishing an exposition or even a commentary on the *Theaetetus*. Hence I shall not study in detail the long discussion wherein Socrates develops and criticizes Protagorean relativism in all of its forms and aspects—individualism, social relativism, pragmatism. It is all very interesting, very instructive, very modern; but it would carry us too far afield and would lead us astray from our goal.

Let us then return to the argument of the *Theaetetus*. Alongside the negative criticism of Protagorean relativism, the self-refuting criticism just referred to, we find also a positive criticism different in type, a criticism by the facts. Indeed, Protagorean relativism implies or affirms the nonexistence of all being apart from sensation, of any object not viewed through a subject. Our science, on the other hand, includes, or sets itself forth as including, such be-

[8] Is the interpretation given by Plato to Protagoras's doctrine just? We cannot say, for we know very little about it. It is possible that Protagoras taught not individualistic sensationalism, but a sensualistic anthropologism, a sort of common-sense philosophy (the real is what is perceived as the object of sensory perception), directed primarily against his contemporaries's magical-religious concepts or superstitions.

ing; it includes prevision, that is to say, affirmation regarding the future; it concerns itself with objects that do not depend upon us, since future events happen or not without regard for our convictions concerning them. Thus, as regards the future, man is not the measure of things, quite the reverse; "things" are the "measure" of man and of the objective rightness or wrongness of his pretended "science." In addition, and this is perhaps still more important, the future as such is not the object of sensation, but of thought. And not only the future; for even in the present and, moreover, in present perception there are a host of things which are neither grasped or even sighted by sensation. Actually, perception is not sensation; it is something much more complex, wherein the multiplicity of sensations properly so-called is unified and organized in the subject, that is, in the soul. Thus, it is not the senses that perceive, but the soul through its sensory organs. Not the senses, but the soul grasps the significance of the words we hear—as Theaetetus observed at the very beginning of the dialogue, yet without realizing all the implications of his remark. Finally, it is still the soul that apprehends what is common to two or more domains of sense data, to wit, their being, number, resemblance or dissimilarity, identity or differences. General ideas have not, like sense data, any real organs. It is the soul itself and by itself that appears to examine general ideas in all objects. And that is why, Socrates informs us, "as soon as they are born, and by a gift of nature, man and beast have the power of sensation for all impressions which make their way through the bodily canals to the soul. But the reasonings which confront these impressions in their relationships with being (essence, οὐσία) and with the useful are finally developed in the persons in whom the act takes place only by effort, with time, at the price of great labor and a long apprenticeship." Since one cannot attain truth if being, or essence, is not attained, and since no science can be found where truth is absent, it follows that "science consists not of impressions, but of reasoning on impressions . . . in the act, whatever name it bears, by which the soul applies itself singly and directly to the study of being."

The name of this act, Theaetetus tells us, is "judgment" or "opinion." Without being too dogmatic about what is only a working hypothesis, he therefore proposes to identify science with opinion; not with any kind of opinion, however, for this may be true or false, but with true opinion (δόξα ἀληθής).

The definition of science as true opinion is banal and current enough. Socrates makes an equally banal and current objection to it, typical of the eristics, concerning the impossibility of false opinion or judgment; in other words, the impossibility of error.[9] What it amounts to is this: either one knows a thing or not; one cannot be ignorant of what one knows, or know what one is ignorant of, any more than one can confound knowledge with ignorance, or being with nonbeing; what is with what is not. But the object of the false judgment is therefore what is not; now, what is not is nothing, and a judgment concerning nothing does not even amount to a judgment at all. We see clearly, then, that false opinion is impossible, a conclusion one can also perceive more simply by pointing out that one cannot be wrong about either what one knows or what one does not know, and that one cannot confuse what one does know with what one does not know.

Be that as it may, false opinion is a fact; one cannot doubt that error exists. How explain its presence in thought? But, first, what is thought? "A discourse the soul holds by itself and at length on the object it examines," . . . explains Socrates,[10] "to think is naught but to enter into discussion with oneself, to address oneself questions and answers, passing from the affirmative to the negative. When the soul has come to a decision, whether slowly or pre-

---

[9] The problem of error is one of philosophy's very serious and crucial problems.
[10] How can we not recall to mind in this connection Descartes, who in his retreat, in 1619, "held conversation with himself about his thoughts"?

cipitously, and thenceforth remains constant in its affirmation and doubts no longer, that is what we take for an opinion. So this act of judgment is what I would call 'discourse,' and opinion is discourse expressed not orally and to others, but silently and to oneself."

This Socratic description is a fine one—we note in passing that it explains the *raison d'être* of the dialogue [11] but does it help us determine the point where error creeps into our minds? Perhaps, on condition that we thoroughly understand the description; that we know how to decipher it; and see what Socrates is trying to show us.

But let us return to the problem of error. Error, Socrates tells us, cannot be produced when the soul in judging is "in contact" with the objects on which the judgment bears, where those objects are "present" to thought. Thus, no one can confuse the Even with the Odd, the One with the Other, Good (in itself) with Evil. But error may take place when one of the terms of the comparison is present without the other; in cases in which, for example, the sensation present is interpreted by the aid of memory, which contains and preserves traces of past impressions, "as if they were in the soul an indelible wax" on which they would be inscribed and engraved. Recognition of an object present would thus consist of fitting the present sensation into the old imprint formerly made by it; but these imprints are more or less distinct, varying with the quality of the wax; moreover they deteriorate with time. Consequently, it sometimes happens that the imprint is not assigned to the right compartment; that, and nothing else, constitutes false recognition or confusion.

A beautiful theory, indeed, and most enticing to Theaetetus. Unfortunately, it does not explain cases in which error creeps in apropos of nonsensible objects, such as errors of calculation,

[11] Thought is the soul's dialogue with itself.

where the problem is not to count present objects, but to add the numbers themselves, which are obviously not objects of sensation, but of thought.

The physiologic theory of memory, with its oversimplified image of imprints upon wax, having proven inadequate, Socrates undertakes to sketch another and subtler one, calculated to bring us finally to understand how it is possible "not to know what one knows." But to do so we must first make our notion of knowledge more precise. Is it not "presumptuous," remarks Socrates, and the remark is of the utmost importance, to wish to discuss knowledge before knowing what science is? An eristic would forbid us the use of these terms and would reproach us with our vicious manner of arguing. And he would be right, for "many a time, indeed, we have said 'we know' and 'we don't know' as if we understood each other, when actually we still know nothing about science." The vicious circle is apparent, and, unfortunately, inevitable. When a disconcerted Theaetetus asks, "But how will you argue, Socrates, without using these terms?" Socrates replies, "So far as I am concerned, it would be impossible for me to argue without them."

But let us go on. To "know," it is said, means to possess science. It is better to say "to possess" science rather than "to have" it; that permits us to introduce into the domain of knowledge the distinction between actuality and nonactuality, presence and nonpresence, which we used to differentiate sensation and memory. Indeed, we possess many things we cannot lay hands on—thus, a suit one has acquired but is not at present wearing is still possessed. Similarly, everything one has learned, all the science one has acquired, are possessed, stored away somewhere in the memory, even when one does not think of them, even when one does not call them to mind. Thereupon Socrates likens memory to a sort of aviary, wherein a bird trainer would place in reserve all the birds (sciences) caught in the hunt. He possesses them in his birdhouse, without, however, having them at hand. He may take them out, but in doing so, he can make a mistake and seize one bird in place of another—a ringdove, for example, instead of a pigeon. Just as when we search our memory for the sciences which we have stored away and which we possess—another way of saying the things that we have learned and know—it happens sometimes that we make a mistake and instead of seizing what we are looking for, we lay hands on something else.

At first glance this explanation of error, or "false opinion," appears satisfactory; but only at first glance, for it implies that ignorance is a function of knowledge—a paradoxical and disastrous consequence.[12] If, as Theaetetus proposes, one were to place in the birdhouse "nonsciences" helter-skelter with "sciences" (so that we would call it a mistake when instead of a science we caught a nonscience), not only would this presuppose a solution for the problem of error, but we would in fact be brought right back to our starting point.[13] For he who in catching a nonscience (in place of a science) would formulate a false opinion, would still think he was formulating a true opinion, and would thus be confusing science with nonscience. So the eristic, resuming his former arguments, would throw the old question at us again: "Is it possible to know one and the other, science and nonscience, and still mistake one for the other?" If in order to explain error we were to say that the distinction between science and nonscience is the object of another science of a higher type, then we would have to construct a new birdhouse, and so on *ad infinitum*.

The identification of science with true opinion (or, inversely, of true opinion with science) renders false opinion impossible. But the existence of false opinion was our point of departure in defining science as true opinion. We have, then, arrived at a formal contradiction; the dialectic study of Theaetetus's hypothesis has resulted

[12] One can be mistaken only in what one knows, in what one has learned.
[13] The nonsciences being errors, the solution proposed by Theaetetus therefore presupposes the existence of error as of something positive.

in its self-destruction.[14] We may therefore conclude that science is not true opinion and that true opinion is not science, which incidentally furnishes an immediate explanation for the possibility of error or of false opinion. Besides, we ought to have been able to realize this directly, much more rapidly and simply. Every day the persuasive eloquence of the rhetoricians gives rise to all sorts of opinions in those who listen, without, however, teaching them anything. It even happens that in a lawsuit the judge, persuaded by their arguments, forms a true opinion and pronounces a correct sentence on the basis of facts, the science of which is beyond his ken.

But what then is science? A new effort at definition appears necessary, and Theaetetus suddenly remembers having heard someone say something on the subject which had escaped his recollection, but which comes back to him now—to wit, that "true opinion accompanied by reason (δόξα αληθής μετὰ λόγου) is science, and unaccompanied by reason lies without the realm of science. Thus, things about which one cannot reason would not be the object of science— that is just the way the thing was put."

The "somebody" to whom Theaetetus alludes is in all probability Socrates himself. Has he not informed us in the *Meno* and elsewhere that opinion (δόξα) differs from science in that the former is weak and unstable and cannot give an account of itself, but that strengthened and linked with reasoning, it becomes science? Hence, some critics have estimated that the formula employed by Theaetetus—science is true opinion accompanied by reasoning—serves to recall an authentic Platonic definition belonging to a preceding period or stage of Plato's thought and subsequently discarded.

[14] The destructive reasoning appears fairly sophistical, it must be admitted; and one sometimes wonders that Plato put it into Socrates's mouth, thereby utilizing it as something worth while. If we are astonished, it is because we do not take sufficient cognizance of the fact that this reasoning is simply *ex hypothesi* from the identification of opinion with science. Indeed, if such identification be admitted, the conclusion becomes banal, for "false opinion" then means "false science."

The Theaetetus

According to this theory, Plato in the *Theaetetus* answers, corrects, and criticizes himself.

For my part, I believe nothing of the sort. Quite the reverse, I believe with some other critics that Plato is concerned either with shelving an apparently analogous doctrine (of Democritus, in all probability) or of preventing a possible misunderstanding of his own view, not to be confused with that of Democritus. Indeed, the formula criticized by Plato is not identical with the one he puts in Socrates's mouth; young Theaetetus's memory has deceived him, or else he has misunderstood. Hence, Socrates feels that the theory alluded to by Theaetetus is identical with the one he has "dreamed of," according to which everything in nature is composed of certain simple elements (στοιχεῖα) that form, so to speak, its letters: the "composites," the "syllables" and the "words" are according to this theory the object of λόγος and therefore of science. As for the elements, or letters, nothing can be "said" about them; they can only be apprehended by sensation (αἰσθητά); inexpressible, they are ἄλογα and remain thus indescribable, beyond the scope of discourse or reason. All of which amounts to saying, in more modern terms, that every composite necessarily entails nondefinable or "irrational" elements and that in every composite the structure or form is the object of reason and consequently of science. The theory is highly plausible. But it is difficult to admit, argues Socrates, that the elements with which an intelligible complex is composed are themselves beyond the scope of reason; [15] that if, on the contrary, one were to deny that the "syllable" is composed of letters and if one treated it as a simple formal unity, this would itself be an element and hence an ἄλογος; besides, and here we have a factual objection, do we not learn letters before syllables, and is

---

[15] The elements of an intelligible ensemble, the ideal composites of an idea, must be and are intelligible, although undefinable. No element, not even if purely sensible, is absolutely ἄλογος, since it can be distinguished from others and identified with itself. Plato's criticism of relationism is extremely suggestive.

learning them aught but knowing how to recognize them and distinguish them one from the other? [16]

But to pass on to a more important problem, let us see, in general, "what is meant by this λόγος (reason or discourse), which, coupled with true opinion, engenders the supreme perfection of science." Λόγος means, first of all, discourse; to add discourse to true opinion is simply to give it verbal expression; which, so far as we can judge, does not change its nature, in view of the fact that any opinion is capable of being thus expressed.

To add λόγος to true opinion may also mean to add to the global —and hence vague—knowledge of a thing, the knowledge of its structure and of the elements that compose it.[17] Thus, we quite understand what a chariot is, but we could not enumerate the one hundred pieces which, according to Hesiod, compose it; he who could, would have the scientific knowledge, while we would have only an opinion. That is an interesting conception, affirms Socrates, and such a λόγος no doubt adds something to the current opinion one has of the thing. But can that be called science? Certainly not, for before it can be so called the one who knows all the component parts of the chariot (or all the letters of a word) must be able to recognize them even if they form part of any other assemblage (or are found in another word). Knowing how to enumerate in the desired order the component elements of an object does not, then, imply that one has scientific knowledge of it.[18] In other words, there is a λόγος, which does not transform true opinion into knowledge.

Finally, a third and last sense of the term "true opinion" designates "the difference (διαφορά) which distinguishes each object from all others." But true opinion is already supposed not to limit

[16] The theory of irrationals elaborated by Theaetetus demonstrates that in fact these so-called irrationals are not irrational at all.
[17] The elements must themselves be objects of science.
[18] Knowledge by acquaintance, the practical knowledge of the artisan, is not science.

The Theaetetus

itself to vague generalities, and it must be able to distinguish the object it concerns itself with from all others. If it could not distinguish Theaetetus from Theodorus or Socrates, how could it assert anything true [19] of Theaetetus? What, then, does the addition of λόγος signify? The addition of a judgment or true opinion concerning the distinguishing features? How perfectly ridiculous! If one were to say that what one has in mind is not adding one opinion to another, but rather adding the science of the difference to true opinion, one would doubtless avoid being ridiculous, but on the other hand one would find himself faced with an irremediably circular definition.

We have reached the end of the dialogue, and the conclusion follows that the discussion has led nowhere. Theaetetus has nothing more to say. He has been entirely delivered, and all that he brought forth was wind. Socrates has the last word, telling Theaetetus that if, purified by the ordeal undergone, he were ever to try once more to conceive, he would probably produce something better. For the time being, Socrates must be off; he has to appear at the Royal Portico to answer the accusation Meletus has drawn up against him.

The renewal of the discussion on science will never take place, as we are all too well aware. Socrates will not be able to lead it; and so we shall never know what science is—unless we already know. Unless we are able from the discussion that unfolded before us to draw a positive conclusion, one that Theaetetus, who did not understand Socrates's lesson and did not comply with his orders, was not able or did not know how to draw.

So Theaetetus did not understand the lesson and did not follow Socrates's injunctions? Quite right! And here, again, we can understand why—Theaetetus is too young. Philosophy is not for youth; the mathematician is precocious; the philosopher is not. Theaetetus has no experience in philosophic research. He is too modest and does not dare make the effort to think for himself de-

[19] It could not state anything false, either; it could not state anything.

manded of him by Socrates.[20] His pregnancies were false, and none of the progeny he produced were his own or the fruit of his own reflection. They were naught but opinions—false opinions at that—culled in the course of his readings or conversations. So in conversing with Socrates he had plucked them from his memory, rather than from the depths of the soul, where lies true science, a reminiscence of reality perceived and possessed by the soul.

Then, too, it may be that it was not his fault. We always begin by error, by forgetting ourselves, and we must destroy the error before we can turn to the truth it was masking. That is why it was necessary to purge young Theaetetus's soul, to empty it of the opinions that encumbered it and that prevented it from seizing hold of the truth already possessed. The encumberment of opinions amassed until they blind the soul—is this not the very thing that struck us at the beginning of the dialogue, when we saw Theaetetus furnish Socrates with a marvelous example of really scientific reasoning, while at the same time he was unable to answer his question, What is science? All Theaetetus had to do to furnish a correct answer was to tell us exactly what he had just done; not only did he not do so—he is incapable of exercising reflective thought, he has not learned the γνῶθι σεαυτὸν—but the falsity of the answer he does give us is all too obvious. Is there, indeed, anything farther removed from sensation than the study of numbers, particularly of irrational numbers and their relationships? Is that not the best refutation of sensationalism? We realize it clearly, but it is farthest from Theaetetus's mind (and the subtle elegance of Plato's dialogue is such that he does not have Socrates point this out to him). He has often read and has often heard it said by his master Theodorus that science is "sensation"; he, in turn, repeats it. But Theodorus, while still a young man, has given up "abstract

[20] At the moment, he is both too inexperienced and too modest. Only for the moment, for later he will succeed in making this effort. Then he will become a philosopher.

questions" to devote himself entirely to geometry, and out of friendship for Protagoras has adopted his epistemology. Theaetetus repeats it, as later he will repeat that science is true opinion, or true opinion accompanied by reason.

As a mathematician, however, accustomed to the rigorousness and precision of mathematical demonstrations, he ought immediately to have realized—as we did—that the science they give us (which may be the foundation of a judgment or of an "opinion") is something quite different from an opinion, true or false, that can be with or without foundation and quite different from a conviction that may have seized hold of the soul. Socrates's beautiful description comparing thought to discourse, to a dialogue the soul engages in with itself, ought to have been enough by itself. Is it not clear that the discourse the soul addresses to itself and by which it convinces itself to adopt one or the other opinion may just as well be a "persuasive" or even sophistical discourse as a scientific piece of reasoning? Once we understand that opinion is not science and that consequently true opinion is no different in this respect from false opinion, we immediately understand the possibility of error, of confusing true and false opinions. How, indeed, could we distinguish true from false opinion without first knowing what truth is, that is, without possessing science? Thus, all this study of opinion presupposes science, without which it cannot be pursued.

As for the dilemma arising from the brutal opposition between knowledge and nonknowledge, science and nonscience, the dilemma onto which the eristic claimed to be impaling us, how could Theaetetus not have understood from the start its artificiality and falseness, accustomed as he was to solving problems and demonstrating theorems, that is, drawing the conclusions implicitly contained in a series of propositions, axioms, or hypotheses? To know what one does not know, not to know what one does know! We who were present during the dialogue in which the Socratic obstetrics drew from Theaetetus knowledge ignorant of itself, we who like Euclid and Terpsion have read or heard the *Meno*, know full well that, far from being impossible, it is the normal, real, or even essential situation of human beings.

To know what one does not know; not to know what one does know. To know; to have science. What does it all mean? Here, again, is something that we know without knowing it. Theaetetus did not understand the lesson, the profound meaning of the Socratic criticism of his third and last definition of science. It is crystal clear, however, and we felt it coming to a head throughout a good part of the discussion during which Socrates led us to realize that in our research we used the terms "science" and "knowledge" as if we already understood them; he even told us that this was inevitable; that at least he, Socrates, could not act otherwise. Hence we were not too astonished to see Theaetetus come out in the end with a circular definition. What else could he end up with, when the whole discussion had been moving in circles from the beginning? His only mistake was not to realize it, not to understand that the necessary circularity of every definition of science reveals to us the pre-eminent character of this notion. To define it is quite as impossible as to "define" the notion of Being or of the Good.

How, then, can we know what science is? In precisely the same way that we know what being is. Besides, Socrates has told us expressly: science is nothing other than the possession of truth. And truth is nothing other than the revelation of being. We have science when we are in truth, that is, when our soul, in immediate contact with reality, with being, reflects it and reveals it to itself. This being, this reality—must we repeat?—is not the disorganized mass of sensible objects that the populace (and the sophist) call by that name. Being in the popular sense, mobile, unstable, and transitory, is not, or is barely, being; it is and it is not, at one and the same time, and that is why it cannot be the object of science, but at best the object of opinion. No, the being that we envisage is the stable, immutable being of essence that our soul has in its possession, a possession it now recalls to mind, or at least that it can so recall, which can thus be made present itself to the soul.

The apprehension of being in its essence, structure, and relations (and it is clear that one cannot understand it without effectuating such an apprehension) or, and it amounts to the same thing, the revelation and expression of being by discourse and truth—that is what we mean by science and reason. And the operation of the soul which leads us toward this apprehension is what we call reasoning.

Is not that the very goal pursued in his domain by the mathematician Theaetetus? And is that not what our master Socrates teaches us in a much more general and more profound way when, breaking and destroying the outer shell of error and of opinion that envelopes the soul and holds it trammeled, he opens or reopens for it the road to truth which leads to being?

That, no doubt, is what Euclid and Terpsion said or might have said to each other as they listened to the dialogue *Theaetetus*. That is what readers of this astonishing work ought to say to themselves. That—and many other things which I leave them to formulate for themselves.

May they then reread, as they no doubt will, the Socratic dialogues of Plato, making sure in each one to take the part of the reader-auditor. They themselves will find there the answers that Socrates supposedly refused them. And at the same time they will see a very tight-knit doctrine taking shape, that one might call the doctrine of the diversity of natural aptitudes, a conception, likewise tight-knit, of philosophic teaching or education (for Socrates represents and incarnates philosophy) as the sole means of differentiating between these aptitudes, the sole means also of developing the worthy ones, the sole means, in brief, of selecting and training the true elite, intellectual and moral, of the State.

The problem is with us today, as immediate and as pressingly important as of old. For want of a solution, ancient Greece succumbed under the blows of the Macedonian barbarians. And for an inadequate solution we ourselves have also nearly been overcome.

Politics

POLITICS AND PHILOSOPHY

THE PROBLEM of politics is one of the most important in the thought and works of Plato, as everyone knows. And this is not at all surprising. Rather, the contrary would have been astonishing. For no Greek, especially no Athenian, would ever have been able, even had he so desired, to dissociate himself from all interest in political life,[1] least of all, no doubt, the young aristocrat Plato, the son of Ariston, destined by his very birth to the responsibilities and service of the State.

But one could go farther and aver that Plato's entire work is concerned with political preoccupations; and that the problems we have studied so far—the problem of the dialogue, the problem of the teaching of philosophy, the criterion for judging and the means of training the select—are also basically political problems. Indeed, is the political problem, that of the constitution and government of the city, anything other than the ethical problem of the elite who govern, in other words, the problem of that "political virtue," the importance of which we have glimpsed in the *Meno* and the *Protagoras?* If that is so—and it is so for Plato—the philosophical problem and the political problem are one and the same.[2]

How, indeed, could it be otherwise for him, if it is true that his entire philosophical life was determined by an eminently political event, the condemnation and death of Socrates, which steered

---

[1] Participation in political life was considered by the Greeks a freeman's privilege, their very own prerogative which distinguished them and set them over and above the barbarians. As a consequence, no other people has ever concerned itself with politics to such an extent as the Greeks, who established, or tried out, all types of possible and imaginable constitutions and, not content with that, succeeded, alone among the peoples of antiquity, in formulating a political philosophy.

[2] Inversely, the political problem and the philosophical problem are equally one and the same.

toward speculative thought the energies that otherwise, perhaps, would have been consumed in action.

Plato's meeting with Socrates fired his soul and kindled in it a philosophical spark. The impression produced by Socrates, the unforgettable memory of Socrates, nourished the flame which still lights our way today. Yet Socrates, the sole true philosopher the world has ever known, Socrates, the friend of the gods, the best and the wisest of men, was condemned to death by his fellow citizens.

Was it the result of chance? Of a concomitance of unfortunate circumstances? Of political intrigue? Of inept defense? No doubt all these played their parts. But Plato would have had to be a very bad philosopher, indeed, to have satisfied himself with such explanations.

No, the condemnation of Socrates was inevitable and full of meaning. Socrates *had* to die just because he was a *philosopher*. He had to die because there was no place for him, for the philosopher, in the city.

How, then, should one live, and what should one do? Flee? But where to—it is the same everywhere. Retire from the city where everything goes inevitably from bad to worse, where lying, vanity, the glitter of false appearance dominate and oppress justice, truth, and good? Become a stranger to it all? Take refuge in private life, in study, in contemplation? That is one possible solution to the problem, in fact the classical solution, the one which the Epicureans and Stoics adopted in diverse forms, the one which Aristotle was to adopt. And Plato himself, in a celebrated passage of the *Theaetetus*, depicts the philosopher

who knows not the road to the public square or where the tribunal, the counsel hall, and all the other public halls of deliberation in the city are located. He has neither caught a glimpse nor heard an echo of the laws and decrees, their debates or promulgations. Not even in his wildest dreams does he consider taking part in club cabals for winning public office or the meetings, banquets, or revels where flute-players furnish entertainment. The good and the evil that happen in the city, what blemish may have been transmitted to anyone from his ancestors, male or female [3]—of all this the philosopher has no more awareness than of, to quote the proverb, the number of casks it takes to fill up the ocean. Neither is he conscious of his own ignorance; for if he abstains from participation in all such activity, it is not through vainglory, but simply that in reality only his body dwells in the town. His thought, disdaining all such matters as mere pettiness and nothingness, takes flight here, there, and everywhere, as Pindar puts it, "sounding out the abysses of the earth" and measuring their proportions in terms of celestial magnitudes, pursuing the course of the stars and scrutinizing the nature of reality in detail and in entirety without ever allowing his gaze to fall to what is close at hand.[4]

The philosopher who is a stranger in the city, in every terrestrial city, the citizen of the kingdom of the Spirit, citizen of the Cosmos, represents, as we have just stated, a possible solution. Perhaps even the only one possible, if we admit with Herodotus that the city of man is evil and unjust *in essence* and that all the forms of government through which it presents itself to us—monarchy, aristocracy, democracy—merely cover up the same reality, that of tyrannical power. It is not, in any case, a perfect solution. For human life in the complete sense of the term is impossible, as Plato is firmly convinced, outside the city. A god may isolate himself with impunity, an animal, also; but never a man, not even a philosopher.[5]

Is that not after all the lesson of Socrates, who never wished to separate himself from the city—from *his* city—or to violate the law, even the unrighteous law that condemned him, or to flee his chastisement?

[3] This is doubtless an allusion to Pericles.
[4] The classical image of the philosopher is that of Thales, who scrutinizes the stars until he falls into a well.
[5] Hence, only in the perfect city will the philosopher be able to become what he ought to be, a sage. So long as he lives in an imperfect city, in our human cities, he will never be anything but a philosopher, that is, one who pursues wisdom without ever entirely attaining and possessing it.

Again we ask ourselves, what is there left to do if one can neither live in the city nor withdraw from it? There is only one means of escaping the dilemma: the city must be reformed. This will constitute a blessing, as much to the city itself as to the philosopher. For the city that condemns a Socrates is a sick and evil city. It condemns him because, being unjust, it cannot endure the presence of a just man; because, being grossly ignorant, it cannot suffer the presence of a man who possesses knowledge and reveals to the city its own ignorance and unrighteousness. But who can reform the unjust and ignorant city, unjust because of its ignorance, unless it be he who *knows*, in other words, the philosopher? Knowledge, however, is insufficient, as Socrates's example shows. Power is indispensable.

Consequently, the solution of the problem posited by Socrates's death is very simple, even though according to Plato himself it is paradoxical; the philosopher has no place in the city unless he be at its helm. As Plato himself will put it, if human life, a life worthy of being lived, is to be possible, philosophers must become kings, or —and this amounts to almost the same thing—kings must be philosophers.

Power to the philosopher-kings . . . is this idea of Plato's really so strange and paradoxical after all? Is it not, on the contrary, natural enough, or at least reasonable enough, to entrust power to the one who knows how to distinguish between good and evil, truth and error, reality and illusion—to one who knows whether it is good or not to construct arsenals and launch ships, rather than to a man ignorant of all this, to the philosopher rather than to the strategist, financier, or demagogue? Is it not reasonable, likewise, to let the philosopher direct so important a matter as the education of youth, the selection and formation of the elite, the choice and training of the future leaders of the city, rather than to leave such matters to chance, without plan, method, or principle? Has knowledge less right to exercise influence on the direction of affairs than courage, riches, oratorical talent? or even simply birth and tradition?

Politics and Philosophy

Fundamentally the paradox consists, not in Plato's conception, but in the fact that it appears so strange to us.

The idea that the philosopher must be the head or the king of the city forms the basis of the *Republic*. That is where the term philosopher-king first appears. But it is clear that this conception had long formed an integral part of Plato's thought, perhaps ever since Socrates's death. What is, after all, the true statesman glimpsed in the *Meno*, master of political science and hence capable of teaching and transmitting it to his successors, if not a philosopher-king, or the statesman described in the dialogue of that name? And what is this political science, if not the science of good and evil, of justice and injustice—in other words, philosophy?

As early as in the *Meno* and especially in the *Gorgias* where he answers the attack of Callicles who would reduce philosophy to the role of a cultural element and would bar the philosopher from any political action for which he is fundamentally unsuited, Plato pronounces a radical condemnation of all Athenian statesmen and sets up as a model Socrates, the only statesman worthy of the name.

Indeed, Pericles is praised for having brought Athens to the peak of power, for having filled its treasury with money and its arsenals with galleys. But was all that for the good or the evil of the city? Did he leave Athens any happier or, and this is most important of all, any better than he found it? The whole question is there, and the answer is unequivocal.

If it is relatively easy to see that the city must be reformed and even that the philosopher must perform the task, obviously it is far more difficult to accomplish this aim.[6] It may be that in his youth Plato believed it possible to operate directly by immediate political action. But he suffered disillusionment. The evil was too deep-seated, the corruption too far advanced. It was impossible to influ-

[6] One might say that there lies the paradox; in order to reform the city, the philosophers must be invested with power, which could never be attained in an unreformed State.

ence men already formed, already perverted by the unjust city, by the miseducation she had given them. One had to go back a step. The reform of the city—political and moral reform, of course (for Plato morals and politics cannot be divorced)—presupposes and implies a preliminary reform of education. Before reforming the city one must first form its future citizens, especially its future leaders. To be in a position to do this, one must demonstrate, or show, that philosophical training is worth more than any other kind and that the duty and the right of instructing youth and the training and the education of the elite fall properly upon the philosopher. To demonstrate this, among many other things, is one of the aims of Plato's Socratic dialogues.

Let us go through, for example, the *Euthyphron*, or the *Laches*, or the *Charmides*. The *Euthyphron* introduces to us the priest of that name, a man of exemplary piety, a piety such that he does not hesitate to make a capital accusation against his own father, guilty of having left a slave who was a murderer to die in the temple premises, guilty thereby of having sullied the sacred dwelling of the god whom Euthyphron served. And yet Euthyphron does not know how to answer Socrates's natural question whether handing over or even accusing his father is not an impious act in the first place, for, as is readily apparent to the reader, if not to Euthyphron himself, he is totally ignorant of the nature, or better, of the essence of piety. Piety, he repeats, is what pleases the gods. But what pleases the gods? And in the case of a conflict of duties, what path ought one to choose? Euthyphron has no idea; he has never considered the problem. He is perplexed by Socrates's question: do deeds of piety please the gods because they are pious, or, on the contrary, are they pious because they please the gods?[6a] To tell the truth, he barely understands it. To be pious is to do what the gods command; it is,

[6a] This, by the way, is a very difficult problem which became later the crux of the medieval Christian philosophy.

Politics and Philosophy

above all, *to offer the sacrifices and accomplish the rites required by religion.*

It is very clear that the pious Euthyphron has literally no notion of piety, or, if you prefer, his conception of piety is perfectly and absolutely meaningless and has no positive content, for the very simple and very grave reason that he shares the popular and inconsistent view of the gods. Euthyphron is devoted to tradition; he is credulous and bigoted; he believes in myths and in everything the poets tell us; he regards religion under the aspect of *do ut des.*

And the reader understands: Euthyphron knows nothing of true religion, because he does not know, what Socrates knows and teaches, that God is righteousness, justice, and truth.

The *Laches* shows us two celebrated strategists, Laches and Nicias, and reveals their views on the burning question of the education of children.[7] It is natural enough that generals prefer a military career to any other and consequently extol military education above all other types. It is likewise quite natural to see them hostile to modern education, to any innovation, even to all those military innovations that are drummed into their ears. Their ideal is naturally purely traditional, the military training of the good old days that formed "good" infantrymen capable of fighting courageously and resisting the enemy. Unfortunately, the generals do not know what constitutes "goodness" in the soldier any more than they know what makes him courageous; they have never thought about it. They do not understand, although Socrates explains it to them at length, that courage ($ἀνδρεία$) is a moral quality which presupposes knowledge of the real danger, of what one ought to fear above all, that is, knowledge of a scale of values, knowledge of something more precious than life, of a good for which one is willing to die. They do not see, as the reader sees, that true courage, which is

[7] The biting irony of the dialogue is emphasized by the choice of interlocutors, Lysimachus, son of Aristides, and Melesias, son of Thucydides.

something other than simple physical temerity, implies knowing what is good in itself and therefore implies philosophy. And the reader-auditor will perhaps whisper to himself: what a pity that such honest, brave generals should be so stupid; what a pity that they are not philosophers! With a little philosophy, Nicias (the more intelligent of the two) probably would not have led the Sicilian expedition to disaster.

Finally, the *Charmides* introduces us to Plato's young uncle, a charming adolescent, endowed with all the graces of spirit and body, virtuous, modest, and properly brought up. Charmides is the pick of the crop; he represents the *summum* that can be attained by Athenian education. Nothing is lacking in him—nothing save one thing, namely, philosophic training. And that is a failing of the utmost importance.

Charmides is good and virtuous, but he is ignorant of wisdom and virtue. And the reader, who knows Charmides's subsequent career, says to himself: there's the explanation, a purely habitual virtue, unconscious, not buttressed by thought and knowledge. What a misfortune that so beautiful a nature, so richly endowed, should not have been formed by Socrates; what a good man and what a good statesman he could have made of him!

The problem of education was a burning one in Plato's day. The old, traditional education, very simple and rudimentary—reading and writing, gymnastics and music—which culminated in the reading of the poets and ended with ephebic training and military service, was obviously already outmoded. It was adequate to serve the needs of the Athens that was a small semi-agricultural community perched on the Attic hills. It no longer met the needs of an Athens that was a great maritime power, the capital of a vast empire, the commercial and financial center of the Greek world, an Athens whose fleets ploughed up the seas as far as Spain and the distant Crimea. But the new education offered to Athenian youth by the sophist or the rhetorician though intellectually on a much higher

Politics and Philosophy

level [8] was not much better. Or, to be more exact, it was still worse, at least from Plato's standpoint. For if the earlier type of education formed country gentlemen who were fairly unpolished, untutored, and uncouth, it at least produced honest men. But the new type of education offered by the sophists formed cultured and brilliant but immoral seekers of power and success.

The criticism of the sophists had indeed shaken to its very foundations the old, traditional notions of patriarchal morality and had ruined them without setting up anything in their place. Or worse yet, it had, crushing away all social hypocrisy, openly put in place of the old ideal of courage, honor, and devotion to the city, the new ideal of pleasure and power—in a word, the ideal of tyranny, which the enigmatic Callicles [9] of the *Gorgias* so aptly formulates; far better than Nietzsche.

Callicles—*sit venia verbo*—lets the cat out of the bag. He admits that it is only through false pride that the sophists speak of justice and virtue, "to conform to common usage," because people would be indignant if the sophists acted otherwise. But in fact there is a definite ambiguity involved; justice according to law and convention and justice and righteousness according to nature have nothing in common. More specifically, they are diametrically antithetical. According to nature, which alone is followed by the sophist, to be just and good is to be strong, victorious in the struggle for life, that struggle which is the law of all existence. In the language of

[8] Intellectually, the new education, the new culture, was, of course, on an incomparably higher level than the old one. The sophists gave to their pupils a course of "liberal" studies based primarily on literary criticism and—the aim of the education being preparation for a political career—trained them in public speech, in law and in politics. In order to develop their "culture" Hippias added science, Prodicus, semantics, whereas Protagoras stressed the "social sciences."

[9] Alas, we know nothing about Callicles, not even whether he is a real character, a pseudonym or (which is more probable) a creation of Plato's genius, Socrates's counterpart, or, if one prefers, an image of Plato himself, of what Plato would have been without Socrates.

the people, it is to commit injustice, not undergo it—to be the master, to dominate. Make way for the strong! proclaims Callicles.

The beautiful and the just according to nature is exactly the reverse of the wisdom Socrates speaks of; the aim is to nurture in one's breast the strongest passions, not to suppress them, and by one's courage and intelligence to give free rein to the passions, however strong, lavishing upon them all they desire.[10]

All this is not feasible for the common people. That is why the crowd blames those whom it is ashamed not to be able to imitate. It declares that intemperance is shameful, while endeavoring . . . to enslave men more richly endowed by nature, and for want of being able to procure complete satisfaction for its own passions it eulogizes temperance and justice simply through its own cowardice. What, in truth, could be more shameful and baleful than sage moderation for him who is born the son of a king or who finds within himself the necessary force to acquire command, tyranny, supreme power? What, set up above me the rule of the mob, its idle chatter and ready censure, when I can luxuriate in all the good things of life without anyone's saying me nay? And how could such a man not be unhappy if, bound by an ethics based on justice and temperance, he could grant no more favors to his friends than to his enemies, and that in his own city, where he would be master?

The truth that you claim to be seeking, Socrates, is here: the easy life, intemperance, passion, when countenanced, constitute virtue and happiness. The rest, all those phantasmagoria based on human conventions contrary to nature, are simply foolishness and empty nothings.

There is no need to go any farther. It will readily be understood that propaganda for such "heroic" ethics had as much vogue in Athens at the end of the fifth century before Christ as in Europe at the end of the nineteenth century. It is so flattering to pose as a superman, a "master," a "hero," a "king's son."

To tell the truth, the sophists were not solely or even principally

---

[10] To live with intensity, to live dangerously, such is Callicles's ideal.

responsible for the collapse of the old values. The Peloponnesian war, which depopulated and ruined Greece, the war which set the maritime power of Athenian democracy and the military power of Spartan oligarchy against each other, a war which was primarily ideological and social, had played a nefarious role in the matter. Decimated by war, shaken by the revolutions that accompanied and followed it, Greece was ripe for the era of tyranny. The sophists only reveal and rationalize what is.

To the immorality of his time Plato obviously prefers the traditional aristocratic ethics of the past, that ethics of piety, courage, and devotion to the city of which we have already spoken. But let us make no mistake. We must not imagine, as has sometimes been done, that Plato is an impenitent reactionary. Nobody ever insisted more than he upon the fact that salvation did not and never could consist in going backward. No one condemned traditional education more vigorously than he. All in all, no one more than he admitted the strength of the sophist's position.

Indeed, if sophistical education was worthless, if it was harmful because it proposed to youth a false ideal of life, the old education was not worth much because it could not defend its ideal and because the values it incarnated and inculcated despite itself were not conscious and "strengthened" by reason, because its ideal, that of Anytus for instance, was likewise false, or at least impure. Fundamentally, the common man, as much as the defender of the good old days, was in agreement with the sophist. Only they both stopped half way on the road to sophistry. That is precisely why the traditional conceptions had not been able to stand up against the negative criticism of the sophist and still less against the positive view of Socrates.

Plato's criticism of sophistics, his *bête noire*, occupies half his work. The sophist, for him, is the man who teaches the technique and the ethics of success, pleasure, and self-assertion, who denies the deeply allied notions of objective truth and righteousness. Sophistical teaching trains the public orator, that counterfeit of the true statesman, capable of sweeping the mob off its feet by arguments founded, not on knowledge—that would be impossible, for he knows nothing, jeers at knowledge, and denies its existence—but on appearance and passion. The public orator, the politician, is the man of illusion as opposed to reality, the man of deceit as opposed to truth.

The sophist is the counterfeit of the true philosopher, as the tyrant is the counterfeit of the true chief of state. Even more, tyranny and sophistry are inseparable, like philosophy and the reign of justice in the city. Nothing of Plato's political attitude is understandable, in my opinion, unless one sees him on guard against the hideous specter of tyranny, scrutinizing the horizon across which tomorrow casts its ominous shadow. Even his *philosophic* attitude will be imperfectly understood if one does not take into account that for him tyranny and sophistry are indissolubly joined. The sophist it is who paves the way for the tyrant.[11]

Perhaps nowhere in all Plato's work, not even in the *Gorgias*, is this relationship more forcefully affirmed than in the *Republic*, in the speech of the sophist Thrasymachus,[12] who sets forth as distinctly as one could desire the essential opposition between Socratism and sophistics.[13] Thrasymachus, who joins in the discussion on

[11] It is always the sophists who teach the ethics or anti-ethics of success at any cost, of limitless enjoyment, and expansion of the *ego*.
[12] Thrasymachus, whom Plato introduces to us as Socrates's adversary in the *Republic*, is a real character.
[13] The discussion on justice which forms an introduction to the *Republic* is very interesting in itself, but would lead us too far afield were we to analyse it at length. In it Cephalus, a rich foreigner established at the Pireus, the commercial haven of Athens, presents—and his son Polemarchus defends—a "bourgeois" conception of justice, namely, "to render unto everyone his due, not to lie, not to owe anything to anyone, neither money to men, nor sacrifices to the gods." Cephalus, who is a foreigner and does not take part in the political life of Athens, is a just man according to the popular prephilosophic conception of the term, the inanity of which is readily demonstrated by Socrates. He treats Cephalus with much deference—the latter is a worthy man, and it is not his fault

justice which forms the introduction to the *Republic*, recognizes full well Socrates's goal, the final identification of justice, or of any other virtue, with "righteousness," that is, wisdom and health of the soul. Even more than his method of dialectical analysis, Thrasymachus detests his opponent's ideas, his intellectualism, his moralism, all of which appear to him puerile. Justice, virtue—words, naught but deceptive words! In real life there are the strong and the weak, masters and slaves, those who dominate and those who are dominated. There lies the truth, and all the rest is idle chatter. Justice, he tells us, is the right of the strongest.

Thrasymachus's position is, as we see, very close to that of Callicles (without being identical) and implies a doctrine concerning ethics, society, and the State which, although more than twenty centuries old, has made some commotion in the preceding century and is still being heard from in ours. The doctrine proposed by Thrasymachus consists in admitting that the State is simply organized oppression, organized, of course, for the benefit of the oppressor and maintained by his violence, that law, and consequently justice and morals, are only the conventional expression of the real relationship of domination and servitude within the city.[14]

---

that he understands nothing of philosophy. He has the luck to be a foreigner; it is because of that, because he is not a citizen, that he was able to remain "just."

[14] Thrasymachus's immoralism, or if one prefers, nihilism, fairly close to that defended by Polus in the *Gorgias,* is far more radical than the ethics of the masters urged by Callicles. While the latter affirms the right of a powerful individual to expand and dominate, a right founded, in his opinion, upon his estimation of such an individual as "superior" and "better," according to a scale of values founded upon the "nature of things" and in opposition to the scale of values that is perverted by the resentment of the weak (and less virtuous), Thrasymachus squarely denies every notion of intrinsic value and "natural right." For him, any notion of right is but a hypocritical disguise for reality. Callicles does not go so far. In nature, according to Thrasymachus, there is a perpetual struggle between the strong and the weak; the strong devour the weak, unless the latter, through organizing, become the stronger. But it is as ridiculous to speak of the "superior right" of the stronger as it is to speak of the "superior right" of the weaker. "Wolves eat lambs"; the latter defend themselves, if they can. Neither side has any "right" in the matter.

"Dost thou not know," Thrasymachus asks Socrates, "that among cities some are tyrannical, others democratic, still others aristocratic," structural differences which may appear essential, but which are not so in reality, because they are simply the outerwork for the same fundamental situation, the fact that "the strongest element in each city is the government?" "Now each government establishes its laws for its own advantage; democracy establishes democratic laws; tyranny, tyrannical laws, and so forth. By dint of established law, what is advantageous for those who govern is declared just for the people governed, and the transgressor is punished as a violator of the law, guilty of injustice. There, in a word, my dear Socrates, is my view: in all cities justice consists in one thing alone, advantage to the constituted government, which represents power, whence it follows to everyone who knows how to reason that justice is everywhere the same, the interest of the stronger." It follows according to all the rules of evidence that injustice (in its commonly accepted meaning) is far preferable to justice and that tyranny is the supreme ideal of life.

In truth, if life is only a struggle, it is clear that the "just" man —who might better be called weak-minded—will always be the underdog. And if it be organized violence that forms the essence of the State, and if the State be only a system of oppression and exploitation of the weak by the strong, it is perfectly clear that tyranny, the extreme form of "injustice," best brings out the perfection of the State and the happiness of man, at least of the one who attains tyranny.

Of course, social hypocrisy, the resentment and fear in the weak or the masses, combine to condemn the strong man's violence, which

---

Of course, men speak of "rights," but it is pure hypocrisy, skillful window dressing for the forces which alone give any content to these so-called rights. The role of the sophist (Thrasymachus would perhaps say: of the philosopher) is to destroy, through analysis and criticism, just that illusion maintained by social hypocrisy, to enlighten man about himself, to liberate him from "ideologies."

is termed "injustice." But in his heart everyone knows that "injustice" is more advantageous than "justice" and everyone consequently would be "unjust" if he were not checked by fear of punishment. This is quite evident

if one reaches the stage of complete injustice, that carries to dizzy heights of happiness the man who commits it and to the depths of despair those who undergo it without wishing to commit it. This injustice is tyranny which by fraud and violence seizes hold of another man's goods, whether sacred, profane, private, or public, and not piecemeal, but wholesale. For each of these crimes the man who is caught is punished and covered with stigma; these partial offenders are called sacrilegious, slavedealers, housebreakers, despoilers, thieves, according to the injustice committed. But when a man not only steals their property but also seizes hold of their persons and makes slaves of them, instead of being sullied by these shameful names, he is called happy and blessed, not only by the citizens, but even by all who learn of the consummate injustice he has wrought. Those who censure injustice are not afraid to commit it; they are afraid to suffer from it. Hence, Socrates, injustice on a large scale is stronger, freer, more worthy of a master than is justice, and as I said in the beginning, justice consists of the right of the stronger, whereas injustice is a man's own profit and interest.[15]

Thrasymachus's position is very persuasive, with its open and cynical preaching of an ultra-Nietzschean ethics of egotism and immorality. And in the very exposition Plato gives of it, one senses the attraction it must exercise over the ardent soul of youth, over the soul of his brothers Adeimantus and Glaucon, both present to the discussion.

They tell us so themselves, in fact. Nobody believes in justice,

[15] Thrasymachus is of the opinion, with the common man (and a certain number of philosophers—to be exact, of sophists, ancient and modern) that quantity transforms quality. The pirate who infests the high seas, but who operates on a small scale, will be hung. Alexander, however, who infests the earth, operating on a grand scale, will be deified. There is no need to cite modern and contemporary examples.

according to Glaucon, who proceeds to explain as a current doctrine the sophistical thesis of justice as social hypocrisy and sketches an almost Hobbian theory of human society founded upon a social contract.

Men in a state of nature, Glaucon explains, are animated by a desire for limitless enjoyment. They are therefore by nature inclined to seek self-interest and as a consequence to commit injustice to the detriment of others, but not to submit to it themselves. As a matter of fact, they quickly note that there is a far greater chance that they will suffer from it than that they will commit it; hence their convention, according to which, under pain of the gravest punishment, they make it incumbent upon themselves not to commit injustice, in order not to have to submit to it. Human nature, however, is in no way changed or modified by this convention; at bottom, all men prefer injustice to justice, and if they did not fear punishment, if they were sure of being able to practice injustice with impunity, if they possessed for example Gyges's ring to make themselves invisible, they would all conduct themselves like the worst scoundrels.

Oh, nobody cares to admit this, naturally, for nobody wishes to pass for unjust in the eyes of his fellowmen; that would be too dangerous. All men hypocritically praise justice, deceiving themselves, or at least trying to dupe others, and seeking thus to profit by the advantages resulting from a reputation for justice, without renouncing—quite the reverse—the privilege of committing injustice each time the occasion presents itself. In a word, nobody is voluntarily just and every "just" person is just only in public and unjust in private.[16]

That is the way of the world, in Glaucon's judgment. Felicity and honors are won by the man who keeps his injustice under cover and outwardly *appears* just, while the really just man, the one who

[16] Everyone knows that for Socrates, as for Plato, nobody is unjust or commits evil voluntarily. Injustice is always a consequence of error.

Politics and Philosophy

is just without appearing so, falls prey to every misfortune, is treated as an accomplished evildoer, and ends by being condemned to punishment. Hence, it is clear that any reasonable mortal is bound to prefer injustice to justice.

That is not all. It must be added, remarks Adeimantus, that contrary to what Socrates seems to believe, nobody desires justice for itself and nobody deems it a good. Quite the reverse; everyone agrees that while it is praiseworthy and even profitable on earth, and no doubt in the after world, there is something hard and painful about it. Hence we seek to incite children and men to practice the virtue of justice, not by making it appear that the thing is desirable in itself, but by promising the just and the virtuous all sorts of rewards and by threatening the unjust with punishment as dire in this life as in the life to come. It is obvious that even good men do not believe in the attraction of virtue and justice; it is clear that they deem the promises and the threats, in other words, the hope of future good and the fear of future ill, the sole means of getting mankind to accept justice.

This is not Adeimantus's own opinion, any more than it is Glaucon's, but one must yield to the weight of evidence; such is the common-sense opinion of the vast majority of men, if not of all. Thus, if Socrates really wants to score a victory over sophistry and its mouthpiece Thrasymachus, he must show that justice is good and desirable in itself, and to do so, he must tell us what it is.

To define justice—and with it virtue, courage, honor; to establish a scale of values for determining our conduct; to establish or rather to show the essence of good and of being—all that is implied.

What it amounts to is that Adeimantus summons us to concern ourselves with philosophy. So be it; he is quite right. For as we have seen time and time again, it is from and through philosophy alone that salvation can come.

But philosophy is a serious affair and even, as we shall see, a dangerous one. It involves work, discipline, effort, a sustained and constant exertion. It presupposes an exceptionally gifted nature, for which it serves both as a training ground and the crucial test.

The way is long, no doubt of it, and arduous. And even, we know all too well, uncertain. But that is the path Socrates has pointed out to us, and the task he bequeathed is from his deathbed. To shoulder his burden, modifying and completing it, to train through hard, severe, scientific and philosophic discipline the intellectual and moral elite which one day is destined to reform and save the city, that is Plato's aim in setting to work and establishing a "school," the Academy that has been rightly called the first university of the world.[17] Here Plato proposes to form his team and await the propitious moment for action.

One fine day he will decide that the hour has sounded. A young prince, Dion, nephew of Dionysius I, master of Syracuse, appears upon the scene, endowed with an exceptional nature and rare gifts. Dion on the throne, Dion lending his energy to the experiment! Who knows—one might be able to effectuate at Syracuse something far superior to what the Pythagoreans accomplished at Tarento.

The Syracuse venture turned out badly. The short cut proved to be impractical. There is no royal road in politics any more than in science. But Plato does not get discouraged. He will set forth on the long road. The team will be reconstituted. They will prepare, educate, and form themselves. And at their leisure they will work out, if not a plan for action, at least a model, an ideal draught of the ideal city, of the just city, the dwelling place of the just. It will guide us; it will permit us especially to understand and judge the real city, the unjust city in which the philosopher is required to live and to act until the new era sets in. Until—here or in heaven—he joins the just city, of which he is already a citizen.

[17] Socrates, and therein lay his error, addressed the people, everybody, the masses. Plato addresses an elite that he tries to mold by scientific discipline, which Socrates had neglected to do.

THE JUST CITY

The blueprint of the just city is presented in the *Republic*,[1] unquestionably the richest, as it is the most extensive, of Plato's works. It contains everything: ethics, politics, metaphysics, a treatise on education, a philosophy of history, a treatise on sociology.

In our editions, as in our manuscripts, the *Republic* always bears a subtitle: *On Justice*. And the ancient critics of the imperial period, Plato's first editors, asked themselves in all seriousness: what is the principal subject of the book—what is it primarily about, justice or the constitution of the city? Is it moral or is it political?

The question is a trifling one in my opinion; even worse, it is an absurdity. For it reveals in the consciousness of the editors a dichotomy between ethics and politics (which amounts to saying between politics and philosophy), such a dichotomy being the last thing in the world Plato wanted. My critique immediately implies that the object of study is not the State as such. Notwithstanding whatever may have been said on the subject, especially by German critics, Plato is totally free from worship of the State, that curse of modern thought, at least of a certain modern trend of thought. What preoccupies Plato is not the State, but the man; not the city, as such, but the just city, that is, a city in which a just man, a Socrates, can live without fear of being condemned to banishment or to death. Under our very eyes Plato will construct this just city, adopting an assumption of capital importance that implies the radical repudiation of the social philosophy of sophistics, which he

[1] The protagonists of the dialogue are: Cephalus, a rich foreigner established at Athens; his son and heir Polemarchus; the latter's friend, the sophist Thrasymachus; and Plato's two brothers, Adeimantus and Glaucon. The introduction to the dialogue, Socrates's conversation with Cephalus and Polemarchus, is of extraordinary finesse and artistry. I have no intention of explaining the *Republic* here, but only of outlining an introduction to its perusal.

replaces by a conception that for lack of a better term might be designated as "organicistic."

The city, indeed, is not a collection of individuals, but forms a real unity, a spiritual organism, and by that fact there is established an analogy between its constitution and structure and that of man. The analogy makes of the former a real *macranthropos* and of the latter a veritable *micropolis*.[2] Thus, because the analogy rests upon a mutual interdependence, it is impossible to study man without at the same time studying the city of which he forms a part. The psychological structure of the individual and the social structure of the city fit together perfectly, or, in modern terms, social psychology and individual psychology are mutually interdependent.[3]

To turn now to the study of the city, "Let us observe its birth." What does that mean? Shall we attempt to retrace through archaeology and history the real origin of human cities? Far from it. Plato, like all rationalists, has no regard for history or historic science (which is not science, but myth). The critics, fortunately increasingly few in number, who since Aristotle reproach him for not taking history into account and for offering us an inaccurate theory as to the historic origins of the City of Man—in which they are incontrovertibly right—make the mistake of not understanding Plato's goal and method. His method is a constructive one, consciously borrowed from geometric analysis. The genesis of the city as presented by Plato is ideal and hence unreal, almost as unreal, basically, as the genesis of a geometric figure constructed from the simple (abstract) elements which compose it. This ideal genesis does not tell us how the triangle and the sphere came into being; and nobody, I am sure, thinks that the latter was actually engendered by a circumference turning about its axis. In explaining the

[2] These terms are, of course, not platonic.
[3] The structure of the city presents in large characters the same text that the soul presents in small ones. The study of Man has therefore to start with that of the State.

The Just City

genesis of his figures, the geometer does not relate their history to us; he does something different and, from his viewpoint, something more important. He permits us to understand their nature, their essence, their structure. Plato has exactly the same aim; by creating the city before our eyes, by constructing it from simple abstract elements, namely, men, he tries to help us understand its nature as well as to discover the place and role of justice in the State.

But let us begin. "The birth of a city," says Socrates, "is due to the individual's lack of self-sufficiency and his need for a host of things." We note distinctly that the need for and the fact of mutual aid are the bases of the city. Not fear, as the Hobbian theory of social contract sketched by Glaucon would have it, but solidarity is the most primitive, the most deep-seated social tie.[4]

In our city, where the multiplicity of needs brings together a great number of associates and auxiliaries in a single place of residence, we are going to insist upon the division of labor for the obvious welfare of the community. The members of the city will not all do the same thing; that would be stupid and disadvantageous. Instead, they will specialize in their activities and occupations; some will be farmers, others shepherds, artisans. There will also be people engaged in commerce; trade between members of the small city first, next trade with the outside world; so that there will be sailors, pilots, shipbuilders, and others.

Our little city is founded. It can live. Everyone in this city has something to do—that is the first principle of Plato's social philosophy: everyone must do something, must contribute in some way to the life of the city. And it is not enough for them to do merely anything; they must exercise their own particular skill, mind their own business (τὰ ἑαυτοῦ πράττειν); they all work, and everyone may eat his fill. Of course, not fancy food, but that is not important for Plato. Plato has no interest in gastronomy. The health of body and soul matters more to him than pleasures of the palate.

[4] Aristotle will use the term "friendship," φιλία.

The little city founded by Socrates—nothing more than a small town somewhere in Greece or in Thrace—the Rousseauist city of virtuous barbarians, does not have the good fortune to be pleasing to Glaucon. "What!" he exclaims, "call that a human city? Why, it is more like a city of pigs!"

Glaucon's judgment is severe and depicts him, perhaps, better than it depicts the city, which although no doubt imperfect, is nonetheless superior in many respects to real cities. It is a sane city, free from the defects that cause rottenness in ours.[5] But Socrates does not undertake to defend his city. That is understandable; he is not in the least a champion of the "return to nature," or even of the "good old days." A city of barbarians without spiritual life was never Plato's ideal.

Let us go farther. The city grows, becomes richer, and immediately luxury, arts, and vices make their appearance. The enlarged city can no longer be self-sufficient. It must expand its territory; it must then make war upon its neighbors. It must also defend itself against them.[6] From that time on, a new class appears, the warrior class. Faithful to the principle of the division of labor in society, a reasonable principle "upon which we have agreed in founding the city and according to which it is impossible for a single person to exercise several professions properly," we shall entrust the conduct of war to an army of professional soldiers.[7] Arts, luxury, vices, and war—the city is now complete.

But beware! With the warriors a new element of first-rate importance has appeared in our city. The army constitutes a real force, in fact *the force*, the element of power in the city. Thus, depending on the moral nature of the warrior, he will either defend the city against its enemies, or, without waiting for others to at-

[5] Nevertheless, as we shall soon see, defects and vices will be introduced of themselves, as it were, as soon as the city grows big and prosperous.

[6] Plato, a realist, takes into account, in constructing his city, the normal conditions for human existence in his day.

[7] The professional army more and more supplanted the citizens' army in Greece.

The Just City

tack and destroy it, he will seize hold of it and destroy it himself. In other words, he will be either its servant and organ or its master. In fact, in order completely to fulfill his role he must be both. Defender and protector of the city and its citizens, he must also be its guardian (φύλαξ).

The guardian of the commonwealth constitutes the very framework of the State—its soul. It is he who defends it; it is he who also administers it. In the Platonic city there is no separation of powers, which is the normal rule anyway in the ancient State. In peace, as in war, the same people command and hold public power.[8] That is the factual status; it is also for Plato an inexorable result of his method, for the unity of the State presupposes and implies the unity of power and command.

But let us return to the guardian. In the Platonic State he is at the absolute center of everything;[9] so much so that throughout the ten books of the *Republic* the guardian is Plato's sole, or nearly sole, preoccupation. As a matter of fact, Plato seems to think that men are, generally speaking, capable of arranging their small affairs by themselves. It is useless and even, perhaps, ridiculous to wish to organize, direct, and regulate their private, domestic, economic affairs and to teach them to perform their callings. It is enough to watch over them, to see to it that they mind their own business and nobody else's, to see to it also that they do not grow too rich, for great wealth upsets the balance and with it the unity

---

[8] The separation of powers is a modern concept. In antiquity a quite different conception prevailed. The power of command is unified, and those who command in time of peace must be fit to take command in time of war. Thus the great captains of antiquity were civilians who made war and also peace. Decadence began when the military took over civil powers.

[9] Plato is perfectly right; these civil servants, these functionaries, constitute the backbone of the State. A State is only as good as its functionaries. The guardians of the Platonic city make up the corps of its civil and military functionaries. Plato was the first to understand their role and to envisage the necessity of forming them into a special corps with appropriate instruction and training.

of the city that Plato wishes to safeguard above all else. Great wealth contains an element of power; it ceases, thus, to be a purely private matter and becomes a political affair.

Otherwise, one can almost forget about the simple citizens who [10] are entrusted to the care of the "guardians." But it is quite a different story for these guardians, whose function is specifically to attend to other people's business, to direct and to govern the city. They must be chosen with the greatest care. They must be accorded a very special education to enable them to fulfill their tasks. In a word, they must be taught their profession of public guardianship.[11]

To train our "guardians" we shall first exercise the most severe choice. We shall pick them from the intellectual, moral, and physical elite of the city's youth. We shall override any distinctions as to sex. For although woman is, generally speaking, weaker than man, both physically and intellectually, the difference, according to Plato, is not qualitative or one of essence and is not such as to justify us in excluding woman from public life or the service of the city, and to relegate her to the inferior tasks of the women's quarters. And so we shall give them all, including the women, the same very carefully planned education.

Education, the training of youth—we know full well that here is Plato's primary preoccupation. According to him the great crisis of contemporary cities, Athens' great crime, is totally to neglect this task, at least to take no interest in it and to leave it entirely in the hands of private individuals. Sparta's great merit, on the other hand, is in giving its children an education, regulated and controlled by the State, the same for all, and to have it superintended by the city's highest magistrates. Of course, the education in vogue in Sparta is very far from being ideal. Whatever has been said on the subject, Plato is anything but a dyed-in-the-wool devotee of the

[10] Of course, their physical and moral education must be supervised.
[11] The occupation of guardian, not being a specialized trade (outside of military art), this apprenticeship will consist above all of general instruction.

Laconic code, and his program of secondary and higher instruction has [12] nothing in common with the rough-and-ready, unpolished training of the Spartans. But the principle is good and just. It is up to the State to supervise the forming of its future citizens, especially its future guardians, those who will have to watch over it.

In order that the city may be unified, education must be equally unified; in order that it may be just and virtuous, the principles of virtue and justice must be inculcated in all its children from earliest infancy. Nothing is more dangerous than to neglect the children, as is so often done. Plato launches into a violent criticism of Athenian education, which not only—as we well know—fails to inculcate virtue in the young, but even perverts them by teaching them lying, knavery, and cruelty. Indeed, from earliest childhood they are told ridiculous fables about the gods of Olympus, and later they are made to study and even to learn by heart the works of the poets, Hesiod and Homer, which give them a scandalous idea of divinity, presenting gods who make war, gods who lie, cheat, and wallow in voluptuous lust. Fine examples, indeed, to propose to youth! After having studied the story of Uranus and Chronos, or the story of Hera chained by her husband, and other myths, one can hardly be astonished if the young are later lacking in respect toward their parents, if after having learned so many examples of injustice, knavery, and shameless favoritism practiced by the gods, they act the same way when they grow up. And how can one expect them to be brave and ready at any moment to give their lives to the city if they are constantly presented with images painting in blackest colors the survival of the soul in Hades and the miserable condition to which the dead are reduced, or if they are shown as examples the purest heroes, a Hector for instance, dominated and subjugated by the fear of death?

[12] This program, which no doubt reproduces the Academy's curriculum, takes up half the *Republic*.

The first basis of sane education is therefore religious reform, a new and very lofty conception of God. Hence, in the new city we are in the process of constructing, we shall banish all the books, all the fables which do not declare that God is good, and that He is just; that He is absolutely straightforward and truthful in discourse; that He never changes form, never deceives; and that He has a horror of lying. In fact, that is not enough—for the poets relate to us infamous deeds performed not only by the gods, but also by men and heroes. There again we must expurgate such texts, so that our children will have before their eyes only models of grandeur, courage, honor, and virtue.[13]

It is clear that all Greek literature will be banned from Plato's city. At least, what will remain will not be worth much. School editions—*ad usum delphini*. We know the type. Still, the influence of literature on the reader's soul, especially on the tender and plastic soul of the children and the adolescent, can be profound. And it is true that certain great literary works have exercised an evil influence.[14] Be that as it may, for Plato, literary beauty of form does not redeem the immoral contents of poetry. Anyway, the Republic can get along without artists, but it cannot do without citizens, especially virtuous guardians.

The basis of education having been established by moral fables, the next concern is with the child's body and with character training. Body and character training means gymnastics and music. The modern reader will be rather astonished. Gymnastics, of course; but music? What does that have to do with the matter? He will, perhaps, recall that the Greek word for music, μουσική, does

---

[13] Beauty also—the Platonic city will be beautiful, ornamented with statues and works of art. It will be well constructed. Plato thinks, and rightly so, that a virtuous and healthy youth cannot be brought up in the midst of ugliness or in hovels.

[14] Among literary works of no artistic value some have exercised an ill-fated influence. Who can figure out the pernicious influence of the serial novel and of the cinema?

not mean "music," but designates everything that has to do with the Muses, in other words the arts and the sciences, approximately what used to be called "letters" and is now called "culture." That is correct. "Music" is simply "general culture," and a "musical man," μουσικὸς ἀνήρ, means not a good musician, but a cultivated man of letters.

However, in this general culture, purely *musical* instruction plays a prominent role. Indeed, for Plato, as well as for others, music *stricto sensu* is, for the forming of the soul, the exact equivalent of what gymnastics is for the forming of the body. The power of music on the soul yields to nothing but literature. Since the soul is more important than the body, which it dominates or at least ought to dominate, music plays or ought to play an infinitely greater role than gymnastics in the education of the young. Plato therefore devotes a lengthy discussion to the problem of musical education and to the determination of the musical modes that we are going to admit in our State. It is clear that we shall not allow all of them, that only simple, harmonious, virile music will have the freedom of the city and that over-violent music, impassioned music, nostalgic and plaintive chants will be severely banned. How curious to us, all this belief in the formative role of music! Is it the result of the verbal analogy which permits us to speak of a "harmonious" body and soul? Is it something else? That is possible, even very probable. But to discuss this problem thoroughly would lead us too far afield.

Music and gymnastics by no means exhaust the contents of the instructional system, or more exactly of the primary education we shall bestow upon the city's children. They will also have, above all, good literary instruction,[15] moral, religious, and civic education. For, must we repeat, we are in the process of training future citi-

---

[15] Plato obviously thinks that one can make good literature out of good sentiments. Even more; true beauty and good being inseparable, if not identical, great art will necessarily be virtuous.

zens. Hence, by every means and from earliest childhood, neglecting nothing, neither fairy tales, games, nor the myths about heroes and gods, we seek to inculcate in children principles of ethics and religion, respect for law, and above all love of and devotion to the city.[16]

This is the common instruction or education. For the elite, the future guardians of the commonwealth, far more is needed. They will be given in addition a more advanced course of study: they will be taught "letters" and sciences; they will be given good "secondary instruction," so that when they finish their studies they may become really cultured, "musical," men and women.

But we shall not force them to learn, for we are all aware that science, unlike mechanical arts and trade, cannot be taught from without. It is not something that can be instilled by drill. Science is not for everybody. Only picked souls, souls consumed with the desire for knowledge and understanding, are capable of acquiring scientific knowledge.[17]

Their secondary instruction terminated, the guardians embark upon military training and service, or more properly, the service to the State which will last all their lives. At twenty, they undergo a new examination. A new and rigorous selection will pick the best material from whose ranks the actual or perfect guardians (φύλαξ παντελής), the highest magistrates, the rulers and "kings" of the city, will finally be chosen. The rest will become their "auxiliaries" (ἐπίκουροι), soldiers in war and policemen in peace. The chosen ones must be given, or, to be exact, must give themselves, an infinitely more careful and solid initiation into science, a very advanced graduate education, which will last ten years and enable them to obtain a real and profound knowledge of science, in first

---

[16] A city for which its citizens hesitate to sacrifice themselves is a city without viability. In any case, it will not last long.

[17] The aim of instruction is not to instill information, but to form the mind by the functioning of the intelligence. Thanks to the liberty accorded the pupils, the sifting of good from bad operates, one might say, automatically.

line mathematical science. The aim of these ten years of study and research is not, I insist, to grant the city's future magistrates useful or practical knowledge, but rather to make of them savants, scientists, or, as Descartes put it two thousand years later, "to feed their souls on truth." Thus, the course of study aims not at technical instruction, but at intellectual and also moral training.[18]

As a matter of fact, moral training is quite as important as intellectual training for the future governing class, and is not to be neglected. But we can no longer pursue this training by inculcating moral precepts. Just as higher intellectual training is accomplished in and by the actual working of the intelligence which posits or finds problems and seeks to solve them, thereby putting to the test its faculty of discovering and perceiving the solution, so we can exercise the moral sense or the sense of duty of our young guardians, by placing problems, that is, temptations of every sort, before them, thus putting them to the test. Thanks to these tests by temptation, we can determine whether the moral and civic education that we have bestowed upon them has really succeeded in shaping their souls, in impregnating them with its principles, in becoming an integral part of their make-up.

Thus, by a dual series of training and exercises, that is, intellectual and moral tests, after ten years of temptations overcome and scientific problems solved, the picked future governors will prepare to face the last and most redoubtable test, that of philosophy. Not until they are thirty do they approach the study of dialectics. At thirty? Yes, for philosophy (Callicles and Cephalus to the contrary notwithstanding) is for maturity, not for youth. "Today," writes Plato, and there is no need to change a word of this text, "those who pursue this study are striplings just emerged from boyhood, who occupy themselves with philosophy before they study

[18] Basically, intellectual training and moral training are part and parcel of each other. Plato, as we well know, does not believe in the possibility of a divorce between the intelligence and the will. Knowledge is prolonged and fulfilled in action; theory dominates practice.

domestic economy and commerce and leave it behind as soon as they find themselves up against its most difficult aspects; yet it is they who pass for accomplished philosophers. Later they think they are doing a great deal by condescending to attend lectures on philosophy to which they are invited; they are convinced philosophy should be only a pastime. As they approach old age, with minor exceptions, they all fade out much more completely than Heraclitus's sun, inasmuch as they are never rekindled." It is clear, however, that the twilight of life, when violent passions diminish, is just the time when the soul, provided it be well endowed and well prepared, is most capable of contemplating the truth. Wisdom is the appanage of age; *sapientia filia temporis.*

At best, philosophy is an arduous matter. Plato does not cease telling us and repeating how rare the philosophic vocation is, how few and far between are the souls endowed with the gifts necessary to profit by it—memory, intelligence, capacity for work, love of truth, and so forth. Philosophy, he repeats—and it is a constant doctrine with Plato—is not accessible to everybody; it is only for the elite. And even this elite, he tells us, cannot approach philosophic studies and practice dialectics without first having received solid scientific instruction, without first having, through the study and the practice of mathematics, purified the spirit and acquired the habit of turning away from the unstable world of sense to view, beyond, the stability of ideas and mathematical being, accessible to thought alone. No short and easy road to philosophy exists.[19] To teach it, therefore, to youths is not only useless, but even positively dangerous.

Everyone knows, writes Plato, and once again there is not a word to change in his text, that

[19] Thus, to place the teaching of philosophy in the cycle of secondary studies would be, for Plato, proof of the misunderstanding of the very essence of philosophy.

adolescents who have once tasted dialectics abuse the subject and make sport of it and use it only for the purposes of contradiction; following the example of those who confuse them, they confuse others in turn, and like puppies, they take pleasure in pulling apart and tearing to bits with their reasoning all who approach them, thereby making a jest of the most serious thing in the world, critical discussion of opinion and the dialectic pursuit of truth. [Hence] after having often confused their contradictors or having often been confused themselves, they soon arrive at the stage of not believing in anything they used to believe.

Then, incapable of replacing the beliefs that their critical spirit destroyed, they are driven to relativism, skepticism, and sophistry.[20] "That is why," Plato adds maliciously, "eventually they and all of philosophy with them are brought into public disrepute."

Philosophy, let us repeat, is a dangerous thing. It requires courage, perseverance, exceptional gifts; on the proving ground of philosophy comes the acid test. The real leaders, the philosopher-kings of the Platonic city, will later be chosen from among those who by dint of long-continued, patient efforts finally reach the truth, the contemplation or intuitive knowledge of the Being and the Good.

Later—but for the time being they will re-enter the ranks and in order to acquire experience of men and things will serve the city for fifteen years in subaltern positions as "auxiliaries" to the wise "philosopher-kings" who constitute its supreme council. Fifteen years of practical activity, fifteen years of meditation, fifteen years of being put to the test! At last, at the age of fifty, the best among them, exerting still another effort, will prove capable of attaining the goal so patiently and so methodically pursued.

At the age of fifty, those who have survived and have distinguished themselves from every point of view and in every subject, both in their

[20] The "debunking" that was all the rage between the last two wars is not, as we perceive, exclusively modern.

work and in the sciences, must be urged to complete their task and open their mind's eye, to elevate their outlook toward the Being who gives light to all things. Then, having seen the Good itself, they will in turn use it as a model in ruling the city, individuals, and themselves for the rest of their lives, devoting the greater part of their time to philosophy; but when their turn comes, boldly confronting the turmoil of politics and taking command in succession, with the public welfare as their sole aim and less as an honor than as an indispensable duty. After having tirelessly trained other citizens according to their own model to replace them in the guardianship of the State, they will pass beyond to the Blessed Isles. The city will consecrate monuments and public sacrifices to their memory, conferring upon them the title of divinity if the law authorizes it, otherwise the title of blessed and divine souls.

We see that in the city of Plato, in this just city for which we are constructing the model or, better yet, tracing the blueprint, knowledge alone justifies the exercise of power, justifies it and at the same time carries with it the moral obligation to exercise it.

The wise philosophers-kings of the Platonic State would, of course, very much prefer to be left alone in order to pursue their studies in peace and lead a purely "theoretical" life. But they know they have no right to do so. They know they owe the city, this city thanks to which they have become what they are, the sacrifice of giving up the pure joy of the disinterested pursuits of knowledge. They know they owe it to knowledge itself. They know that the prisoner, escaped from the cave where he had only shadows to gaze upon, once out in the clear light of day, before the vision of reality, must not keep his discoveries to himself—cannot refuse to go again down into the cave to bring the other prisoners less favored by fate a reflection of the light he has contemplated.

The "guardians" of the Platonic city—and we now understand far better than at the start why they bear that title, for the city has entrusted itself to their care—the "guardians" properly so-called,[21]

---

[21] The complete guardian, παντελὴς φύλαξ.

The Just City

the philosopher-kings, quite as much as their military and civil auxiliaries, are mere servants of the city, pledged to defend her and to protect the public welfare. They are naught else,[22] which explains the mode of life Plato has assigned to them.

The guardians form the city's permanent army, the permanent army of order and welfare. That is why they live like every permanent army in a state of perpetual mobilization, in special dwellings, as it were, away from the houses of the other citizens.

They have not, that is, cannot and ought not to have, any other interests apart from the city as a whole, any other passion than that for its welfare, any other love than that of the city. For that reason they have neither family nor home nor any private possession, and for fear lest they still might become corrupt—the fateful acquisitive passion is powerful in man's heart [23]—Plato forbids them not only to possess but even to touch gold and silver. The city feeds them, clothes them, and arms them. They have everything in common, including women (there can be no permanent marriage [24] for the guardians, men or women), including also the children, who will all be brought up in public nurseries and will not know their fathers, mothers, or brothers, in order that the exclusive affection that each of us is inclined to feel for *his* family, for *his own* people, should not harm the friendship and camaraderie that links them all together or weaken the devotion they owe the city.[25]

---

[22] They are, of course, the servants and the adorers of truth and righteousness, and by that right they are the "guardians" of the city.

[23] Good men, in Plato's system, are not plentifully provided with the world's goods. On the contrary, the possession of goods is incompatible with serving righteousness.

[24] We must not imagine this communal status of women as synonymous with sexual promiscuity; marriage exists, but is of short duration.

[25] The possessive instinct exemplified by "I" and especially by "mine" is the chief enemy. Consequently power should be entrusted only to those who are free from all special, egotistical self-interest. Otherwise, abuse and corruption will always and necessarily exist.

To sum up, remarks Adeimantus, they will resemble mercenaries, and Socrates agrees. But, continues the young man, if they lead the sort of life we have just described, they will not be happy. It is clear that the guardians' life of poverty and hard work, lacking luxury and all personal ambition, appears unattractive to the young people around Socrates. That may be, he replies. But it is of no importance. For it is not the happiness of the guardians that we have sought to bring about in constructing our city, but that of the city as a whole.

We must not forget that the guardians do not dominate the city; they serve her. The whole is always greater than the part, even the noblest part.[26]

Then, to be sure, is it true that the guardians will not be "happy"? Enlarging upon Socrates's reasoning, one might affirm quite the reverse, that they will be perfectly happy, since having only one love, the city, and not being men like ourselves, but in a sense civic virtue incarnate, they will be perfectly content in feeling their duty accomplished.

Perhaps there is no need of going so far. After all, what are the guardians of the commonwealth giving up? Wealth, luxury, and personal ambition. But they do not give these things up outright; they give them up in return for power, honor, the respect and affection of their fellow citizens, and the friendship of their peers. They give them up, not as benefits to which they cannot aspire, but on the contrary as things of little value, unworthy of them. They give them up, as in every true asceticism—affirming their own superiority.

History shows us that man is quite capable of giving up much

---

[26] That is the difference between the true aristocracy, or government by the best citizens, who command and govern only for the *good* of the governed, never for their own self-interest, and any pseudo-aristocratic rule (feudal, oligarchic, demagogic, etc.) in which the governing classes pursue their own self-interest in governing, just as Thrasymachus explained to us.

The Just City

more for much less.[27] Thus, one may hold the opposite view from Adeimantus and argue that the guardians of the Platonic city will be perfectly happy.

Adeimantus's objection is therefore valueless. Doubtless the "normal" or "average" man will never accept the ascetic existence of a public guardian. But Plato has never dreamed of imposing it upon him. The ranks of the guardians are not composed of "average" men. Rather, they form an elite, set apart, educated, and molded with the utmost care. As for the others, so much the better if the life of the guardians is unattractive to them, they will respect them all the more and feel no envy.[28]

One question crops up, however. Can we get the far more numerous classes of merchants, artisans, peasants, and others, who form the economic groundwork of the city, to accept the autocratic power of the order of guardians? For we must not forget that the power must be accepted, not superimposed.[29]

Plato feels, perhaps over-optimistically, that a good education, provided it be really good, that is, such as we have described, will permit inculcating in all members of the city a correct notion of the true and natural hierarchy of values—respect for the best, respect, above all, for knowledge.

In fact, the hierarchy of the Platonic city is arranged according to the degree of knowledge. As we have already said, but the point bears repeating, the wise philosophic magistrates are apt and worthy of the obligations of governing the city just because they

[27] One has only to recall the monastic orders. Indeed, the "guardians" of the Platonic city form a sort of ascetic order of warriors directed by a group of men in whom perfect wisdom is realized, that is, in which sainthood is allied with science.

[28] Once again, Plato is right. The true aristocracy should be poor, which implies that it cannot exist in the city of money and that the wealthy classes can never constitute more than a pseudo-aristocracy, in point of fact, a cacocracy.

[29] Refusal to accept the power of the guardians would automatically disrupt the spiritual unity of the city.

possess knowledge, the true and supreme intuitive knowledge of the good and of the being. Their science radiates out in some way upon the entire city, making it participate as a whole in knowledge. The philosopher-king represents contemplative science of the intellect ($νοῦς$). The other guardians, their aids and auxiliaries, do not go so far. Reason, discursive thought ($διάνοια$) analysis and synthesis constitute their special domain. The plain citizens are satisfied with faith and with the true opinion ($πίστις$ and $ὀρθὴ\ δόξα$) that the savants inculcate in them.[30]

Thus, some possess truth by itself. To others, incapable of perceiving and receiving truth in its purity, it is parceled out in diverse forms, attenuated, weakened, imbedded in the imagination, or reduced to the form of symbol and myth.[31] Thus, to promote unity in the city, all its members will be indoctrinated with belief in the myth of autochthony. Plato is obviously of the opinion that men can be made to believe anything provided it be repeated often enough and begun early enough.[32] They will then be made to believe that they all, or at least their ancestors, are children of the very soil of their fatherland (or mother country, as the Cretans put it), that consequently they are all brothers, still, that different materials were employed in the constitution of each of them, to wit, gold, silver, brass and iron. The brass and iron race forms the mass of the people; that of silver, the class of auxiliary-guardians; the golden race, rarest and most precious, being that of the philosopher-kings.

The three races, or to be more exact, the three classes of the

[30] We are all aware that so far as action is concerned, true opinion is practically the equivalent of knowledge.
[31] One of the most important political tasks of the philosopher guardians is precisely to translate truth accessible only to pure thought into myth accessible to the imagination. That is likewise the role of art, whence the necessity to supervise it.
[32] There, again, modern political reality emphasizing the role of propaganda justifies Plato. Man is a credulous animal, not a reasonable one.

Platonic city, are not in any sense castes. Plato, like everybody else, believes in heredity. He believes, then, that normally the children of guardians will be worthy to succeed them. But he knows all too well how often the descendants of eminent parents disappoint the hopes held for them. Accordingly, in the city directed by philosophers, heredity creates, not a right, but simply a favorable presumption. In fact, the guardians whose function it is, will soon discover superior material among the children of the brass and the iron race, whom they will quickly appoint to the rank of guardian; or, on the contrary, they may discover a nature of brass and iron among the descendants of the elite and direct it to the life of the fields or the shop.

Our city, now, is completed. It is exactly as it must be. It possesses all the virtues that a city is capable of having. It is wise, courageous, temperate, and just. But in fact what constitutes its justice?

Before answering this important question, we must first determine the "seat" of the other three virtues. It is clear that the seat of wisdom is found in wise governors and that we have attributed it to the entire city simply because of them. It is equally clear that the seat of courage is found in the heart of the city's auxiliary-guardians. As for temperance, not only does it include the whole body of society, but it may even be considered the proper virtue of its productive classes.

But justice? It really seems as if there is no room left for it. That is, unless, having no seat of its own in one of the classes or elements of the city, justice consists specifically of order, harmony, the natural hierarchy, and the division of labor founded on it which rules, organizes, and unites the whole city.

Justice has begun its reign in the city almost without our being aware of it, without our expressly having introduced it. It has been realized there because without our taking cognizance of the importance of the step, we decided to construct our city by applying in a rigorously systematic manner the great principle of over-all aptitude. We attributed to each man the most appropriate role and function, or, to put it the other way around, we have assigned to each citizen the role and function which best suited him.[33] And we have automatically, as it were, brought about the order of perfection and justice in the structure of our city, where by that very fact a just hierarchy reigns, founded on the nature of things. Truth to tell, it is exactly the same with man. The human soul, as we well know, is a counterpart, or an exact image of, the city. It, too, is tripartite. In effect the νοῦς, reason, or intellect corresponds in us to the wisdom governing the city. The θυμός, the soul's passionate and spirited faculty, seat of wrath and courage, of pride and violence, corresponds to the warrior class; finally, desire, carnal appetite, avidity, thirst for possession, and concupiscence, correspond to the masses.

The reign of justice in the soul consists, then, of hierarchic order and the subordination of its parts one to the other, a subordination that assures the harmony and perfection of the whole. In a just soul, reason, science, governs, decides, and commands the irascible and impassioned element, which is what sways the appetitive element to obey the dictates of commanding reason.

Justice is exactly that. That is why it is also the soul's health; not only in the figurative sense in which we speak of moral health but also in the strictest and most literal sense of the word.[34] Conversely, injustice, which consists of the disorder and perversion of the natural hierarchy, is the soul's malady.

The Platonic theory of the tripartite soul is both banal and

[33] In that way the maximum personal happiness and the maximum social cohesion are brought about.
[34] Philosophy is therefore a veritable medicine of the soul. The philosophical statesman is thus the city's physician, and that is why, as the *Statesman* explains to us, he could if necessary dispense with the citizens' consent. The doctor prescribes remedies. He does not ask his patients to agree with him, though he will readily explain to the patient the reasons for his action.

The Just City

curious. Banal because it reproduces the popular conception of the division and localization of the soul's faculties—head, heart, and stomach—and curious in its insistence upon the primary importance and the essential role played in the composite human being by the impassioned, spirited element, by the heart. Plato's ideal is not apathy, not a soul without passion or wrath, without fire or flame. The soul of a Stoic sage would seem to Plato incomplete, imperfect, and impotent.[35] Besides, it would form a man lacking in courage, and a man lacking in courage cannot become a "philosopher" or even be a leader.[36] That is why Plato's "guardians" start out in life as soldiers and remain such all their lives.

The perfect city, or at least the plan of the perfect city, is there before our eyes. But what is the perfect city in reality? Is it something that can be made to come true in this world, or is it a dream, a castle in the air, a pure utopia? Not an easy question to answer. It is evident that the just city does not exist and has never existed in our world. In that sense, then, it is a utopia, or more properly an atopia, since it exists only as an idea in the intelligible realm, where ideas have their "existence." Is such a city impossible? Quite impossible, in one sense, since ideas can never come true as such on earth. In the so-called "real" world there are neither circles, triangles, nor straight lines, only the images, participations in and approximations of ideas are there encountered.

Yet one wonders if that is sufficient answer and if the carrying out of the perfect city is not purely and simply a contradiction in terms. Plato manifestly does not think so. The city, as we have constructed it, is not self-contradictory, nor is it incompatible with human nature.[37] For this reason its existence or realization, al-

---

[35] It is curious to observe the perfect agreement on this point between Plato and Spinoza.
[36] A timid soul is the soul of an oligarch or of a slave.
[37] Unless one deems the very existence of the philosopher-kings an impossibility. In effect, the philosophers of the Platonic city are not, strictly speaking, philosophers; they are sages. Wisdom, as the *Statesman* explains to us at length, is

though extremely difficult and consequently extremely problematical, must be considered theoretically possible. It will be possible for the perfect city to become a reality, and it will become one, "when at the head of the State there are found one or more philosophers who, scorning the honors of the times and deeming them unworthy of a freeman and completely lacking in value, will have the greatest esteem for duty and the honors which are its reward and, considering justice the most important and necessary thing, will place themselves at the service of this concept, which will flourish under their efforts until the whole city will be organized under its laws."

Undeniably it is highly improbable that philosophers will ever be chiefs of State—how in the world could they become? Still, theoretically in the course of time every possibility may be fulfilled. It is not *impossible* that a philosopher be born to the purple some day. It is not *impossible* that at the same time others be found to serve him as ministers and counselors. It is true that when one takes cognizance of the program of action these men would have to carry through if they were then desirous of establishing the perfect city, one begins to doubt the practical value of the theoretical possibility just suggested. As a matter of fact, the first measure of the philosophical government of the non-philosophical city will be to

relegate to the fields all those in the State who have passed the age of ten; then they will take their children to shield them from the customs of the day, which are those of their parents too, and they will bring them up in conformity with their own *mores* and principles. This will be the

---

the prerogative of the gods, not of men, and that is why absolute power is just as much a divine prerogative. Conferred upon man, it will always be unjustified and therefore unjust. Consequently there will never be "royal" power in man, but always tyrannical power. The *Laws* will even tell us that absolute power is so out of proportion to human nature that its possession necessarily leads man to mental aberration—in which Plato is obviously right. But perhaps all that only applies to real man.

quickest and the most expedient means of establishing the aforesaid constitution in a State that will be happy and will overwhelm with honors the nation of its birth.

Nothing easier, no doubt—unless Socrates (this, too, is not impossible) is gently poking fun at his young friends. Be that as it may, it matters little whether our city can in fact ever come true. We know that it is possible in the abstract, and that knowledge must suffice both to guide our action and to aid us in understanding and judging the imperfect cities in the midst of which fate has cast our lot, to form and to determine the ideal structure of Man, to which, in any case, we have to conform our own being.

IMPERFECT CITIES

THE IMPERFECT or real cities are classified by Plato into four main categories, not chosen according to the external juridical structure of their constitutions (such as hereditary government, electoral government, or government by lot), but rather according to their internal structure, the principle they embody, the scale of values that rules them and dominates their life. Accordingly, Plato's study of imperfect cities, containing some of the most beautiful pages he has ever written, does not outline comparative forms of constitutional law, but constitutes a chapter in philosophic anthropology and describes the essential types—moral and social—through which human life is realized in society.

The perfect city is the one in which, in the State, as in man, reason governs, and through it the good, which it contemplates. The imperfect cities are those in which this natural hierarchy is perverted, where the place of reason, or better, knowledge, synonymous with duty, is usurped by some other factor—ambition, avarice, search for pleasure, vanity, or crime.

In his analysis of the imperfect types of city Plato uses a method, or, if you prefer, a manner of presentation, analogous to that used in his general preliminary study of the city. There he had outlined the pseudo-historic origin; here he relates to us the story of the decadence and the progressive degradation of the perfect city.[1] A theoretical history, of course; its phases do not necessarily coincide with those of real history.[2]

The types of imperfect cities are presented to us by Plato in order of descending perfection, or if one prefers, in order of ascending perversion. First timocracy, or the city of courage and honor; next oligarchy, or the city of money and avarice; then democracy, or the city of disorder and anarchy,[3] finally tyranny or the entirely perverted city, the city of fear and crime. Thus, we have two extremes of government—two absolute forms of government, the philosophic city of dominant reason and the tyrannical city of unchained desires—as well as three intermediate forms that all result from the gradual relaxation of natural hierarchy and internal discipline, as from the contamination of the superior forces of the soul (and the leading groups of the State) by its inferior powers, and the men who represent them.

The decay of the perfect city (considered as real) is inevitable— *errare humanum est*—and at some time the rulers of the city will err in selecting the guardians. Men of brass and of iron will rise to superior positions.

From that time everything will go from bad to worse. Instead

---

[1] The myth about decadence permits an explanation of why imperfect cities preserve traces and vestiges of justice and virtue. Thus, what the sophists explain as being due to an effect of social hypocrisy, Plato "explains" by the myth of decadence.

[2] It is clear, for example, that it is not necessary for each city to go through the whole cycle. Athens was never Sparta. Tyranny, as Aristotle has already remarked, can supplant oligarchy directly without passing through the phase of democracy. We have witnessed recent examples of this.

[3] It must never be forgotten that Greek democracy had pushed the principle according to which "anybody any time can be put anywhere" to the point of determining magistracies by lot. This explains some, not all, of the criticism Plato directed against it.

Imperfect Cities

of thinking only of the city, of its welfare and that of the citizens whom they are supposed to protect, the guardians—henceforth unworthy of that title—will look out for themselves, and, no longer satisfied with honor and the sense of having fulfilled their duty, they will seek honors and will wish to obtain the material enjoyment of the pleasures and goods of this world. Instead of remaining the servants of the city, they will try to become its masters, and once the revolution has been accomplished,[4] they will seize possession of the goods and riches of their fellow citizens, whom they will reduce to serfdom, and after having divided up their lands among themselves, they will form above them an hereditary caste of warrior-lords. The perfect city, philosophic or aristocratic, is no more. In its place we have a military State like Sparta or the Doric States of Crete. In those States philosophy, science, culture of mind and soul are no longer held in honor and so are no longer pursued. The training and discipline of the body are the sole interest of the uncouth, boorish lords of the military State. In the education of the children the preparation for a military career replaces everything else. Or, as Plato puts it, music gives way to gymnastics, while bravery, ambition, and military glory appear as the supreme values and the greatest good. That is why this state structure, which is, after all, simply an aristocracy stripped of aristocrats,[5] is called by Plato "timocratic," or "timocracy," government by honor ($\tau\iota\mu\dot{\eta}$), or, better yet, by ambition.

As for the timocratic man, he is, as always, a miniature edition of the city, a man in whom the irascible, impassioned, and irrational elements of the soul have gained the upper hand. He is, therefore, hard and cruel and scorns the science and philosophy he is

[4] No revolution entirely suppresses the previous State, and that is why the timocratic city will keep some traces of the aristocratic order.
[5] The characteristic of aristocracy being devotion to superior values and to the service of the city (the one implies the other), no city worthy of the name can get along entirely without an aristocracy. If aristocracy entirely disappears, the city (*polis*) becomes tyranny.

incapable of understanding. No longer possessed by the thirst for knowledge, he is prey to the thirst for honor, or rather honors.

We realize that the timocratic city is a most unjust city—a city where a philosopher is quite impossible. Although Plato, more than anyone else, knows and appreciates its faults,[6] still he feels that the timocratic city is the best in the world. That may seem strange, yet it is understandable. Courage and honor, although far from being supreme values, are nevertheless real values and far superior to those which rank highest in other imperfect cities. No doubt the timocrat seeks his own honor and his own glory, not, at least not exclusively, that of the city. It is, nevertheless, in the city's service that he finds them.

Alas, the purely timocratic, purely military city is almost impossible, or at least it would be excessively unstable.[7] It cannot even be a stopping point on the way down. Indeed, upon closer examination, it is not the θυμός pure and simple, the impassioned, irascible element of the soul, which revolted against the power of reason: it is the θυμός contaminated and perverted by the appetitive soul, by the acquisitive and concupiscent element in us. How, if that is so, can one expect the θυμός, deprived henceforth of the aid of reason, to resist the allurement of the desire for possession and pleasure? As a matter of fact, the timocratic city is a hypocritical and delusive city, and the timocrat, the man who supposedly appreciates and pursues only honor, or at least honors, in actual fact loves money and pursues wealth. No doubt, he does not so conduct himself openly; officially, he sings the praise of toughness and "Spartan" sobriety. But in his own home he hoards gold and silver.

[6] Nothing is falser than to see Plato as an inveterate admirer of Spartan culture. If he admires (and who does not?) the courage and patriotism of the Spartans, their devotion to the city and the law, neither does he ever miss an opportunity to criticize them.
[7] The Doric cities of Crete are not purely timocratic States any more than Sparta's, but are rather mixtures of timocracy and oligarchy. Generally speaking, none of the types described by Plato can come true in the pure state.

Imperfect Cities

The war-like timocrat is in reality a miser (the avarice and greed of the Spartans were proverbial in Greece). Little by little the man of courage and honor, like his State, becomes transformed into a money-mad man.

The city of money, the oligarchy, as Plato calls it, or the plutocracy, according to Aristotle, and as it is still called today, ranks far below the timocracy in Plato's scale. Indeed, "the more one pursues wealth and the higher the value one places upon it, the less one prizes virtue, for, placed in opposite scales of the balance, they always take an opposite direction." Thus the oligarchic State, in which riches occupy the top rank in the scale of values and money brings honors, power, and the most important offices of the State, is vicious in the fundamental principle of its structure and government.[8] Anyway, may one still speak of a State? Hardly, for the oligarchic city "is not one, but dual, that of the poor and that of the rich, who dwell on the same soil and conspire unceasingly against each other." The city of money, torn by internal strife, and a prey to the class struggle, will therefore by its very nature be a weak State, consequently pacifist. Not, however, through sincere love of peace, but simply through fear, fear of the enemy within, who will paralyze the oligarchic government. Plato explains to us "the almost certain impossibility of waging war on the part of oligarchies, inasmuch as they would be obliged to arm the people, whom they would fear more than the enemy." Besides, last, but not least, "their avarice would prevent their bearing the expense of war."

As for the oligarchic man, Plato does not hide his scorn for him, "he is sordid, makes money on everything, and thinks only of heaping up treasure; in a word, he is one of those whom the multitude praises. Is not such a man the image of the government we have just depicted?" He is doubtless orderly, punctilious, and honest, he leads a settled existence, has no vices, does not go off on sprees

[8] The oligarchy does not serve the State, but uses it for its own personal ends.

or succumb to temptation.[9] But there again, he acts so, not by virtue of a sincere aversion for evil and an equally sincere attachment to righteousness, but solely through meanness and avarice, through love of money and fear of losing it, or even spending it.

Avarice—there is the dominating passion of the city and of the oligarch. Avarice, the thirst for riches, for possessing more, ever more, and with it, of course, the fear of losing the fortune amassed. So the oligarchic city, dominated by the double passion, loses its head, so to speak, and sows the seed of its own downfall. Thus, it does not limit the expenses of private citizens, does not protect the property of the debtor class, and so forth, for it must allow the rich to grow richer. This finally leads to the concentration of wealth in the hands of a few and the establishment of a pauper class —"drones" Plato calls them, the *déclassés* individuals of our modern society, drones, some of whom are armed with stings. It is just this class of impoverished men without possessions which furnishes the leaders [10] of the popular movement that will overthrow the government of the oligarchs. Conspiring alone will not satisfy the poor forever in their feeling against the rich. The day will come when they will rise to action.

The city of money is a sick city, or at least a city that breeds disease. "Thus, a State in an analogous situation falls prey at the slightest provocation to the malady of internal war, while each party makes outside appeals for help, to either an oligarchic or a democratic State; [11] the strife is unleashed sometimes without for-

---

[9] It is curious to observe that luxury and conspicuous wealth are not traits of the oligarchic city. The oligarch is miserly; he desires to possess, not to enjoy, the goods he owns. The passion to spend, contrasted with the thirst to acquire, is, according to Plato, the characteristic of the democrat, who tends to enjoy rather than to hoard. Hence, luxury tolls the knell of oligarchy.

[10] The leaders of the popular revolution are according to Plato invariably found in the higher class. Not so the tyrant, who for his part can come from the lower strata of society.

[11] The interdependence of domestic and foreign politics is not, we see, a new phenomenon. And the fifth column flourished in ancient times as well and for the same reasons as in our day.

eign intervention." Thus, with or without foreign intervention, the revolution breaks out and "democracy is established when the poor, victorious over their enemies, massacre some, banish others, and divide the government and the magistracies equally among those who remain; most often the magistracies are even determined by lot." [12]

If the oligarchic city can only with difficulty lay claim to being a State, in view of the fact that it is actually two, the democratic city has even less right to the appellation, owing to the fact that in it the unity and cohesion which above all else characterize a State, are completely lacking. That is why in Plato's classification of States, democracy occupies an even lower rank than oligarchy.

Plato has no love for democracy, that is certain. Although he does not have the scorn for it which he has for the oligarchic city, he has no sympathy for the democrat, who so far as Plato is concerned is simply the oligarch freed from or deprived of the checks that avarice and fear of ruin imposed on his desire for enjoyment and luxury. The oligarch keeps his desires under control and satisfies only the necessary ones; [13] the democrat, the "drone" we have already referred to,[14] is, on the other hand, the man of all desires, of superfluous ones even more than of necessary ones: "he devotes

[12] The selection of magistrates and even representatives of the people by lot instead of by election appears to us (as to Plato) quite absurd. The Greeks saw in their system a guarantee of equality among citizens and a safeguard against dishonest elections. Let us not forget that we ourselves pick jurors by lot.

[13] Plato in no wise condemns the senses or sensory pleasures. But he does distinguish between necessary, normal desires, the satisfaction of which is indispensable to the happy life, and artificial desires, refinements in the search for pleasure, which constitute a perversion of man's normal attitude. Aristotle's view will be no different.

[14] It is very important to realize that "the democratic man" is not the representative of the people of artisans, farmers, and so forth, which in the corrupt city perpetuates the tradition of the healthy, working city, but is rather the "drone," the impoverished oligarch who has become by that very fact the enemy of oligarchy; the professional politician who seeks a career in politics (and a fortune); the demagogue; and finally the son of the oligarch who, emancipated from parental discipline, endeavors to satisfy his long-suppressed desires.

to superfluous desires as much money, trouble, and time as to necessary desires."

If he be told that some pleasures spring from good and noble desires, and others from perverse desires, that the former must be honored and cultivated, the latter repressed and mastered, he answers only by a sign of disdain and holds that all are akin, to be honored equally.

In brief, he knows neither order nor constraint in his conduct; his mode of life is for him an agreeable, free, and blissful regimen which he has no inclination to change.

Plato feels no more drawn toward democracy than toward the democrat. Maliciously he exercises his verve and wit to point out the disorder that reigns in a democracy, the lack of discipline,[15] the instability, the cult of incompetence, the relativism, and the indifference to public welfare which permits anybody at all to attain governmental powers in the city. For in a democracy, men hold no respect whatsoever for public authority, which explains how magistrates and rulers are appointed "without consideration for the studies by which a political figure has prepared himself for state administration, while it is enough that he call himself a friend of the people for him to be overwhelmed with honors." [16]

True, the constitution and the "mode of life" in a democracy appear at first glance extremely attractive. Indeed, is it not true that "in such a State, a man is free, and that liberty reigns supreme along with freedom of speech, and license to do as one wants"?

Alas, of all governments, or more precisely of all systems of government (or of nongovernment), democracy is the most unstable, the weakest, and the least enduring. Just as in the case of an oligarchic State, its very principle, or if you wish, the almost inevitable exaggeration of its principle, drives it to its own destruction. Indeed, "the goal that was set up and which helped to establish the

---

[15] A recent author has defined the democratic spirit by the formula "the citizen versus the powers that be."
[16] Demagogy is for Plato the democratic city's special ill or vice.

oligarchy was excessive wealth. . . . The insatiable passion for riches and the indifference that it inspires toward everything else cause the ruin of oligarchy." Similarly the insatiable desire for what democracy regards as its supreme good—liberty—causes the ruin of this form of government.

Nothing is more beautiful, more profound, or more timely than Plato's passages describing the birth of the tyranny inevitably engendered by the intoxication of democracy incapable of self-discipline.

Liberty is the supreme good of the democratic city.

"One will hear it said in a democratic State that it is the most beautiful of all and consequently the only State where a man born free can dwell." [17] "Yet the insatiable desire for this good, combined with indifference toward everything else, transforms such a government and obliges it to have recourse to tyranny." "For, when the democratic State . . . becomes intoxicated with pure liberty . . . the spirit of liberty penetrates everywhere, and it soon degenerates into lack of discipline and anarchy. . . . All these accumulated abuses have serious consequences, that is, they make the citizens so touchy that at the least appearance of constraint they grow angry and revolt, and (this is common knowledge) go so far as to mock the written or unwritten laws, so that they may have no master at all." [18]

In so doing, they fall into the power of the demagogue first, then of the tyrant. "For it is certain that every excess generally brings on a violent reaction . . . and in governments more than anywhere

[17] In Pericles's famous speech on Athenian democracy, democracy's superiority to all other types of government is summed up to the fact that in a democracy everybody participates in affairs of State, which means that all its citizens are truly free, and that, from this fact, the selection of the picked leaders of government is conducted freely according to talent rather than wealth or birth. In other words, for Pericles democracy brings about and generalizes true aristocracy. For Plato, Periclean democracy spells the collective tyranny of Athens over its allies. And Post-Periclean democracy succumbs through demagogy.
[18] No political system needs discipline and obedience to law more than democracy.

else." That is why "excess of liberty leads only to excess of slavery, both in individuals and in States . . . and from extreme liberty is born the most complete and atrocious slavery." [19]

To understand fully this process, one must have clearly in view the social composition of the democratic city. It is approximately the same as that of the oligarchic city, the people, the rich, and the "drones," with this difference, however, that in the oligarchy the people have nothing to say, while in a democracy "the people, that is to say the workingmen and the individuals . . . who have only small holdings, form by reason of their number the most powerful class," and that the "drones," despised and kept out of magistracies in the oligarchy, form in the democratic State the class most hated and scorned by Plato, that of professional politicians, leaders and flatterers of the mob, whom they incite to all sorts of iniquitous measures against the rich in order to be able to "despoil them of their fortune and divide it among the people, with the greatest part for themselves." The propertied classes try their best to defend themselves, first by legal means, which endeavor ends in failure and nets them only the accusation of conspiring against the people and being for oligarchy, next by illegal means. The conspiracy, at first imaginary, becomes real, and now it is the people who fall prey to fear. Thenceforth fear will determine the whole subsequent evolution and will dominate the entire life of the State.[20]

The people are afraid. Hence they set up a leader, a protector, as a defense against the maneuvering of the oligarchs, and this protector being a butt for their attacks, the people will give him a guard, an armed force to defend and protect him.[21] From then

[19] Tyranny is born of disorder and anarchy. We have witnessed the aptness of this observation.

[20] We have seen that it is solidarity rather than mutual fear which forms the ultimate basis of the city. But in the depraved city, fear finally succeeds in supplanting solidarity. The sophists are therefore wrong in their social philosophy because they consider a state of decadence a normal state.

[21] The colored-shirt wearers of modern tyrannies.

on the city is lost. The protector of the people, a budding tyrant, in the beginning is all smiles and salutations for everyone he encounters. He protests that he is no tyrant, makes all kinds of promises, both in private and in public, to all and sundry, proclaims a moratorium on debts, and divides up the landed estates among the people, especially among his favorites. Although he affects benevolence and sweetness toward all, he cannot stop there. "When he has finished off his internal enemies . . . he will not cease to provoke wars, in order that the mob should need a leader . . . and also that the citizens, impoverished by taxes, should be forced to apply themselves to their daily tasks and conspire the less against him. Next, as discontent begins to spread, he will finally suppress all who might prove dangerous to his power, even his former friends. Then, after having strengthened his personal guard by the addition of mercenaries and ruffians, he will throw off the mask of benevolence," and tyranny will be revealed in all its horror.

Tyranny is the government of fear and crime, corruption and bribery; the tyrant rules by fear, but he also falls prey to fear.[22] He fears the people, who hate him and whom he oppresses. But he also lives in fear of his own bodyguard, whose only attachment to his person is through the lure of personal profit. Thus, he is constantly obliged to buy anew their uncertain fidelity by loading them with gifts and money. Once he has exhausted the public treasury, he turns to private wealth, and finally he overburdens the people with his extortions. Thus it is that the people by their desire (as it is said) to avoid the phantom of serfdom, bear the yoke of the hardest and bitterest slavery, submission to slaves and even to "the slaves of their slaves."

As for the tyrannical man, he whose praises the poets sing when they vaunt "tyranny as a thing that sets men on a par with the gods," he is actually far from being a superman or from enjoying superhuman happiness. On the contrary, all we have to do is to use

[22] Light has recently been shed on the primordial role of fear in the tyrannical city, by Guglielmo Ferrero, in *Power,* New York, 1943.

the method of analogy which has served us so well up to now, to arrive at diametrically opposed conclusions. The tyrannical city is, indeed, necessarily a poor city, enslaved and preyed upon by fear. It follows that the tyrannical soul is equally poor and starved, gripped by fear and filled with servitude and abjectness.[23] Contrary to what the people believe, the tyrant is not free to do as he wishes—is not the master, but "the slave of his slaves." And similarly, the soul of the tyrant is not free, but subject to his passions and tyrannized by them. The tyrant's soul is incapable of governing itself, having no self-control. It is dominated by its lowest element, by the ferocious beast that lurks in each of us.[24] This is not only a flagrant perversion and a mortal ill for the soul but also an eminently unhappy state. For the tyrannical man is as much less happy than the "royal" man, the aristocrat, or the philosopher, as the tyrannical city is less perfect and therefore less happy than the ideal and just city. And Plato, who amuses himself by calculating this difference in figures, reaches the conclusion that the just man is seven hundred and twenty-nine times happier than the tyrant.

All that is very well, it will be said. Still, tyranny does attract men, while philosophy attracts them very little, indeed. Might it not be, by chance, that the pleasures procured by tyranny attract us because, while doubtless of lower nature than all others, they are yet more powerful, or more intense, and for that reason they enslave us? The objection seems serious and in conformity with common experience. And Plato's response, founded again on his

[23] The Nietzschean heroes extolled by Callicles and Thrasymachus are revealed as possessing a servile soul.

[24] The human soul, according to Plato, is not "naturally" good; or, more exactly, there is in the human soul or nature an element which is passionate, ferocious, savage, and perfectly amoral; our dreams give us sufficient proof of this. That is one of the reasons for the importance attributed by Plato to education: the wild beast which lurks in every one of us must either be dominated by reason or chained by training. There is no need to insist upon the kinship of this Platonic doctrine with certain recent theories about the unconscious.

Imperfect Cities

doctrine of the tripartition of the soul, is most curious and most profound.

Let us recall, he tells us, that we have distinguished three different faculties in the human soul. "We have recognized one by which man knows and one by which he becomes impassioned; as for the third, it has so many different forms that we have been unable to affix to it any unique and appropriate name, but we have designated it by its most important and predominant feature; we have called it the friend of money"; and we may add "that its pleasure and love are dependent upon profit. As for the spirited element . . . it never ceases aspiring with might and main to domination, victory, and reputation." We have also observed that three classes or types of men correspond to these parts of the soul—the philosopher, the ambitious man, the mercenary man. There can be no doubt that each of these types extols as the highest value the one corresponding to his particular psychologic structure and lauds as the highest and most intense pleasure the one procured by satisfying the tendencies and aspirations of the element of the soul that predominates in him.[25] But ought we to believe them all equally? Plato's answer is a negative one, for two very closely interlocked reasons. First, it seems that generally speaking it is reasonable to have confidence in the philosopher's assertions, that is, in those of the man whose proper function is to search and know the truth, rather than in those of an ambitious or tyrannical man. In addition, and this is the principal argument, the philosopher knows the pleasures and satisfactions procured for us by money or ambition, but the ambitious or miserly man does not know the satisfaction that comes from the exercise of reason or the happiness conferred by justice. The philosopher speaks, then, of what he knows through experience; the others, of what they know only through hearsay.[26]

[25] The relativistic error is to put them all on the same level.
[26] The unfortunate result is that the satisfactions philosophy accords the philosopher, while of higher caliber or deeper than all others, have very little chance of attracting souls which by nature are foreign to philosophy.

Conclusion

We have almost reached the close of our study. We see now with perfect clarity that justice is truly the soul's greatest good, that the just man is in every instance infinitely happier than the unjust. We have understood that for man, as for the city, health and happiness consist in being ruled, governed, and dominated by reason, that is, by what is properly speaking divine in us, and that the supreme misfortune for man, as for the city, lies in tyranny.

Now the menace of tyranny is not theoretical; quite the reverse, it is very real. The growing demoralization, the insidious propaganda of the poets, the teaching of the sophists, the demagoguery of their pupils, the public orators, everything combines to propel the mob, ignorant and blind, toward the rule of tyranny. That is why, following the example of his master Socrates, Plato addresses to Athenian democracy a supreme appeal, a final warning: stop where you are on the road to disaster. A little farther, and it will be too late. A little more, and Athens will plunge headlong into the abyss.

CONCLUSION

A QUESTION arises here, in fact a double question: (1) Is the progressive degradation of the forms of political life fatal and irremediable, as Plato seems to have shown us? May one, in general, at least arrest, if not reverse, the movement? (2) Even admitting that this is not impossible, what role can or ought philosophy to play in this salutary undertaking?

The answer to the first question seems readily apparent. It appears to me perfectly obvious that, as I have already stated, the real history of political institutions is not in any sense identifiable for Plato with their ideal history. . . . The latter exists independently of the temporal realm. It reveals to us the internal structure of a certain number of essential forms of society, along with the intimate tendencies which animate or even dominate them. It does not state that a given society, under given conditions, subject

Conclusion

to certain determined actions of equally determined factors, is unable to "skip stages," either forward or backward, or even to buck the current.¹ It tells us nothing about the chronology or the length of the phases described. Thus, to check political and social decay by appropriate reform of the State is by no means impossible, although doubtless extremely difficult.

If such be the case, the philosopher's role likewise stands out in bold relief. What he must do, or at least attempt, is to educate the city, that is, to educate its elite,² to give them or return to them respect for true values, love of justice, devotion to the city, respect for law; to go on with what Socrates began, to accomplish the mission to which Plato devoted his life.

Love of justice, devotion to the city, respect for law; an underlying bond links these things all together. For to be lacking in respect for law, the law which is the very soul of the city, is to put oneself above it, to prefer oneself to the city. Is that not the very height of injustice for a citizen? "The enemy of the law," the anarchist Plato describes for us, the pseudo-citizen of a decomposing democracy, is in the strictest and strongest sense of the term an enemy of the city. The man imbued with anarchy is the budding small-scale tyrant, the forerunner of the large-scale tyrant.

To re-educate the city, to give back to it the sense of true values —doubtless this is a difficult and arduous assignment, full of uncertainty and risks. There, however, lies the task encumbent upon us, that democracy permits us, if not to accomplish—for nobody can foresee the future—at least to hope for and attempt.

Democracy, as we have seen, is a system where anything, or almost anything, can happen. The worst, but also the best. In it one may encounter all types: the sophist and also the philosopher. That is the unique advantage of this way of life, an advantage which in

[1] Athenian history, of which Plato could not very well have been ignorant, shows us that oligarchy can succeed democracy at least for a while, and democracy can establish itself upon the ruins of tyranny.

[2] The example of the elite will inspire the people and strengthen their morale.

Plato's eyes is enormous and that imposes upon the philosopher his role and his place in the combat. Let me repeat: to philosophize and to concern oneself with politics is one and the same thing, and to wrestle with the sophist means at the same time to defend the city against tyranny.

Will the city be saved by the philosophers? We cannot, of course, know the answer. But this much is certain, that therein lies its sole chance of salvation, for the hope nourished in some breasts to see the city reformed and saved by a providential ruler, a "statesman," a πολιτικός, in a word, a "leader," is an absurd and contradictory illusion. Thus the *Statesman* reminds us that knowledge alone justifies the possession and exercise of power and that, consequently, the ideal statesman, invested with absolute power, not limited or circumscribed by law, could never exercise it justly unless he were at the same time endowed with absolute knowledge. It is beyond the shadow of a doubt that a city ruled and governed by a πολιτικός possessed of such a "science," a science that would not be limited to apprehending the general structure of human beings and situations, but would also extend to individuals, would be far happier than a city governed by law. Indeed, from the very fact that law is general, it is never perfectly applicable to individual cases. . . . Alas, such wisdom is not of human stuff. The ideal πολιτικός ought to be a sage, or better yet, a god. If he were only a man, that is, if a man were to place himself above the law, he would necessarily be a tyrant. Absolute wisdom, like the perfect city, is not of this world. Granted man's lot, human imperfections, there is no salvation for man's city without law.

Man's lot, human imperfection! Indeed, we might better have said human perversion, and by that very fact the hierarchy of the types of cities that we have deduced and established in the abstract is turned topsy turvy in reality. We have established the hierarchy of "good" cities: unfortunately, in reality they are all "bad." And as it was later put, *perversio optimi pessima*.

Conclusion 109

Thus nothing is more beautiful in theory than the "royal" city of the all-powerful πολιτικός, but all we have in reality to correspond to it is the infinite abjection of arbitrary rule in the tyrannical State. Nothing is more "honorable" than the austere city of courage and honor, but we know that it is almost as impossible to bring about as the perfect city of absolute wisdom. We know that in reality the counterpart of the city of courage and honor is the hypocritical city, unfaithful to the law, *its law*, the city of the ambitious warrior, who is brutal, vainglorious and greedy—in a word, the worst possible thing on earth, barring tyranny.

Oligarchy, the city of money, is decidedly inferior to the city of courage. Riches are not a "value"; possession is not a principle of union; hence the city of money is weak by nature and divided within itself. In stern reality, it is something else; in reality oligarchy is in no way the city of possession, as it should be according to its law, but rather the city of greed. The oligarch is not the patrician who possesses, but the miser who hoards. Real oligarchy is likewise a perverted city. However, in this case the perversion is in a way less deep-seated: from possessiveness to acquisitiveness is not nearly as far as from honor to vanity. The plunge is not as great when one starts from a lower peak. Hence, real oligarchy, perverted as it is, is in absolute terms less perverted than real timocracy. Besides, being weaker than the latter, it exerts less of an influence upon its citizens, whom it affects less profoundly. It therefore perverts them less. This explains why oligarchy is in fact preferable to timocracy; in actuality, the bourgeois city is more worthy than the feudal one.

The considerations we have just indicated apropos of oligarchy are still more applicable to the democratic city, the city of disorder and of individual opinion. In theory, it is the least perfected of cities, the weakest, the least unified, the least stable—that is precisely why it so readily becomes perverted, crumbles away, and becomes demagogic by turning unfaithful to its own law. But this time the perversion is minor, the fall is but a small one. Real democracy, even when distorted, is still preferable to real plutocracy. Because of its very weakness, it barely influences the intellectual and moral life of the members of the city. Doubtless it does not educate them for the good; but at least it does not systematically divert them towards evil. Finally, the law of the democratic city is itself so amorphous, so far removed from rigidity, that it is the least difficult to bring about in this world of ours. That is why in this world of imperfection and perversion, where the only cities are the "bad" ones, democracy is far and away the best system of government, especially if it achieves self-discipline and does not degenerate into anarchy, the breeder of civil war and despotism.

It is useless, we feel, to insist upon the extraordinary modernity, one could even say the timeliness of Plato's political thought. Nothing bears less resemblance to a modern State than the City-State of the ancients (πόλις) where everyone knew everyone else, around which one could walk in a day. One might as well compare an ancient galley to a superdreadnaught. Yet, as the modern reader peruses those passionate and severe, profound and caustic pages, in which Plato describes for us the decadence of Athenian democracy and its downfall through anarchy and demagogy toward dictatorship and despotism, he cannot refrain from saying to himself: *de nobis fabula narratur*.

The ancient city and the modern city, for all their differences, are both human cities. And human nature, whatever may be said on the subject, has changed but little in the course of the centuries that separate us from Plato; it is always the same motives—the attraction toward the "good things" of life, riches, pleasure, ambition, *honores, divitiae, voluptates*—that impel and determine its passions; it is always the same motives—honor, fidelity, love of truth, and devotion to the good—which guide and enlighten its acts.

That is why Plato's lesson, the message of Socrates that reaches

Conclusion

out to us across the centuries, is pregnant with timely significance for us. Watch out, he warns us. See to the education of the city, of its future citizens, of its future governors. Do not restrict yourselves to training them for a specific job, trade or function: moral education, respect of truth, devotion to the city, is what makes good citizens. Never forget that friendship and the spirit of helpful co-operation form the link that holds the city together and constitutes its force. Never allow discord, fear, and hatred to take root in the State.

Watch out: do not allow distrust of law to gain a foothold and to propagate itself in your city. Distrust for law is the poison that causes the complete dissolution of the State; distrust for law brings on anarchy, which in turn leads straight to tyranny.

Watch out: do not confuse the statesman with the demagogue, the one who enlightens you with the one who flatters you. Trust not the latter; he works not for your good, but for his own. Be on guard: choose carefully those who are to hold the reins of public power; do not let the aristocracy of the public service become transformed into a cacocracy of personal ambition.

In the midst of the crisis that shakes our world to its very foundations, Plato's message is laden with teachings that deserve reflection.

Index

Academy, the, 70, 77n
Acquisitive passion, effects, 85
Adeimantus, 67, 69, 71n, 86
Aeschines of Sphettus, 2
Alexander, 67n
Anamnesis, Platonic, 10n
Anarchy and disorder, 102n; city of, *see* Democracy
Anytus, in the *Meno*, 7, 11, 22, 63
Aptitudes, diversity of natural, 51
Aristides, 12, 59n
Aristocracy, differences between the true and the pseudo-, 86n, 87n; why essential to city: devotion to service and superior values the characteristic of, 95n
Ariston, father of Plato, 53
Aristophanes, 18n
Aristotle, 8n, 54, 72, 94n, 97, 99n
Army, professional, 74; guardians an army of order and welfare, 85
Athens, problem of education, 60, 76, 77; propaganda for heroic ethics, 62
Auditor, spectator, 4; reader, 5
Autochthony, belief in myth of, 88
Avarice, 97, 98; the city of, *see* Oligarchy

Beauty, 78
Being, revelation of, 50
Bentham, 31
Berkeley, 5n
Boileau, 20n

Callias in *Protagoras*, 18n, 19
Callicles of *Gorgias*, 57, 61, 65, 81, 104n
Cephalus in *Republic*, 64n, 71n, 81
Character training with music, 78 f.
Charmides, the, 20, 58, 60
Children, education, 76 ff.; communal status, 85
Christian philosophy, problem of piety, 58n

Cities, philosopher can neither live in nor withdraw from, 54; must be reformed by him, 56; dependence of political and moral reform upon reform of education, 58; structural differences but same fundamental situation, 66; whether the *Republic* is primarily about justice or city, 71; unity and cohesion, 99; whether decadent forms fatal and irremediable: whether the movement can be reversed or arrested: part that philosophy can and ought to play, 106-11; the ancient and the modern, 110
—— the imperfect or real, 93-106; compared with perfect city: method of analyzing, 93; four main categories, 93, 94 ff.
—— the just, 71-93; genesis, 72 ff.; analogy between its constitution and structure and that of man, 72; mutual aid the basis, 73; role and training of guardian and other officials, 75 ff. (*see also* Guardians); hierarchy, 87; three classes in, 88; seat of its four virtues, 89; justice, 89 f.; can the perfect city come true? 91, 109; story of its decadence and progressive degradation, 94 ff.
Command, power of, 9
Common sense and popular opinion, 29
Common-sense philosophy, 38n
Conclusions, inconclusive, 2, 4, 6; of *Meno*, 17; *Protagoras*, 18, 32; *Theaetetus*, 47; political life: the *Republic*, 106-11
Conformism, social, 12n, 13, 24
Courage, 29, 32, 59, 91; timocracy the city of honor and, 94, 96
Cowardice, 32
Crete, Doric States, 95, 96n

Index

Culture as means of character training, 79

Debunking, 83n
Decadence, myth of, 94n
Definitions, use and value of precise, 2
Democracy, Greek, 94n, 101n; or the city of disorder and anarchy, 94, 99-102, 109; its meaning for Pericles and for Plato contrasted, 101n; social composition: causes of downfall, 102; the worst and the best system, 107; why best, 110
Democrat, the, 98n, 99
Demagogy, 100n, 101n, 111
Democritus, 45
Descartes, 17, 20n, 21n, 40n, 81
Desires, normal and superfluous, 99n
Dialectic, Platonic: method, 15n, 29n
Dialectics, study of, 81
Dialogue, or discourse, of soul with itself, 3n, 40, 41, 49
Dialogues, 1-52; the Socratic identified: problems discussed, 1; philosophic, 1-7; why unequaled models of philosophic teaching, 3; acted in Rome in Cicero's time, 4n; Plato's are dramatic compositions, 4 ff.; medieval and modern, not dramatic, 5n; last of the Socratic, 33; exposition of motives for abandoning style of narrated dialogue, 34; demonstration of the need of philosophical training one of the aims of, 58
Dies, A., 37n
Difficulty inherent in the dialogue, purpose, 7
Dion of Syracuse, 70
Dionysius I of Syracuse, 70
Discourse, thought compared to, 3n, 40, 41, 49; what is meant by, 46
Disorder and anarchy, 102n; city of, see Democracy
Division of labor, 73, 74
Doctrine, Socratic, 2, 4, 6; difference between Meno and Protagoras, 18
Doric States of Crete, 95, 96

Dramatic character of dialogues, 4 ff.
Drones, 98, 99, 102

Education, reform of, must precede reform of city, 58; military, 59; a burning question in Plato's day: old and new, 60; Athenian neglect, 60, 76, 77; sophist aims and training, 61n; Plato's primary preoccupation, 76; of city's guardians and other officials, 76 ff.; religious reform the first basis, 78; body and character training with gymnastics and music, 78 f.; intellectual and moral training its aim, 80n, 81; role of philosophy, 81 ff.; Plato's warning to us, 111
Elite, education for public service, 58, 80 ff., 107; addressed by Plato, 70n; guardians (q.v.) selected from, 76
Epicureans, 54
Error, problem of, 40, 41 ff.
Euclid of Mengara, 33, 34, 50
Euthyphron, 58

Family and home denied guardians, 85
Fear, effect upon city, 102; upon tyrant, 103
Ferrero, Guglielmo, 103n
Fifth column, ancient, 98n
Flux, doctrine of, 38
Future, the, 39

Galileo, 5n
Geometric analysis, 72
Glaucon, 67 f., 71n, 74
God, conception of, 59, 78
Gods, evil results of fables about, 77
Good and evil, 29
"Good things" of life, 16
Gorgias, 3, 57, 61, 64, 65n
Gorgias, master of Meno, 8, 13, 15
Government, teaching the science of, 22n; difference between the true and the pseudo-aristocratic, 86n; extremes of: absolute and intermediate forms, 94; *see also* Cities: State
Greece, why ripe for era of tyranny, 63
Greeks, preoccupation with politics, 53n; democracy, 94n, 101n

Index

Guardians, almost the sole preoccupation of the *Republic*, 75; role and training of, 75 ff., 107; selection: women eligible, 76; goal at age of fifty, 83; peaceful study sacrificed for life of service, 84; an army of order and welfare: mode of living: marriage and children, 85; happiness, service and rewards, 86 f.; whether their autocratic power would be accepted, 87, 90n; likened to an ascetic order of warriors, 87n

Gymnastics, 78, 79

Happiness of guardians, 86 f.
Hedonism, 31
Heredity, 89
Herodotus, 55
"Heroic" ethics of the sophists, 61 ff.
Hesiod, 46, 77
Hippias in the *Protagoras*, 18n, 61n
Hippocrates, in the *Protagoras*, 19
History, lack of regard for, 72
Hobbian theory of social contract, 68, 73
Homer, 77
Honor and courage, city of, 94, 96
Hume, 5n
Hypocrisy, social, 66, 68

Ignorance: Socratic, 3; conduct determined by, 31
Imperfect cities, 93-106; *see* Cities
Individual, *see* Man
Injustice, 67, 68n, 90
Intellectual, Meno the "emancipated," 12n
Intelligence and will, 81n
Ironic character of Socratic ignorance, 3
Irrational numbers, 36, 48
Irrationals, theory of, 45 f.

Judgment or opinion, 40; *see* Opinion
Just city, the, 71-93; *see* Cities
Justice (saintliness), 26; sophist belief in justice according to nature as the right of the strong, 61 ff.; discussion on, an introduction to the *Republic*, 64n, 65; whether the *Republic* is primarily about the city or, 71; reign of, in the city, 89; in the soul, 90

Knowledge, remembrance of forgotten, 10, 16, 17; distinguished from true opinion, 13; virtue as, 29 ff.; on how to define, in the *Theaetetus*, 42 ff. *passim;* scientific, acquired only by few, 80; alone justifies exercise of power, 108

Labor, division of, 73, 74
Laches, 58, 59
Law, government by, 108; warning against distrust of, 111
Laws, 92n
Learn, implies to understand, 11n
Lectures, instruction given in, 28n
Liberty, democracy's supreme good yet cause of its downfall, 101 f.
Literary criticism a main basis of sophist teaching, 28n
Literature, pernicious influence of immoral, 77, 78n; not redeemed by beauty of form, 78; great art necessarily virtuous, 79n
Luxury and spending, 98n
Lysimachus in *Laches,* 59n

Magistracies determined by lot, 94n, 99
Maieutic, Socratic, 7
Malebranche, 5
Man, Plato preoccupied with, 71; analogy between constitution and structure of just city and that of just man, 72; capable of arranging our affairs, 75; not "naturally" good: kinship of Platonic doctrine with recent theories about the unconscious, 104n; three types or classes, 105
Marriage, 85
Megaric eristic, criticism of, 34
Megaric school of philosophy, 33n

Melesias in *Laches,* 59n
Meletus, 47
Memory, of forgotten knowledge, 10, 16, 17; physiologic theory, 41; Socrates' theory, 42
Meno, the, 3n, 7-17, 18, 22, 44, 50, 53, 57
Method, preoccupations with, 3
Midwife, 37n
Military city, *see* Timocracy
Military education, 59
Military powers, 75n
Military States, 95
Modernity of Plato's political thought, 110
Monastic orders, guardians compared with, 87n
Money, city of, *see* Oligarchy
Montaigne, 24
Morality: old ideals ruined by sophists, 61; in education and literature, 77 f.; importance: training methods, 81
Music as means of character training: Greek meaning, 78 f.

Natural aptitudes, diversity of, 51
Natural right or justice, 61, 65n
Nicias in *Laches,* 59, 60
Nietzschean ethics, 61, 67, 104n
Nonscience, 43; *see* Error
Numbers, irrational, 36, 48

Oligarchy, or the city of money and avarice, 94, 97 ff., 109
On Justice, subtitle to the Republic, 71
Opinion, defined, 40, 41; popular, 29; true, 13, 15; identification of science with, 40 ff.; linked with reasoning, 44, 49; three senses of term, 45 f.
Orator, public, 64
Oratory, aim of sophist education, 29n

Parmenides, 33n, 34
Parody, Plato a master of, 18
Peloponnesian war, 63
Perception, 39
Pericles, 12, 22, 55n, 57; democracy, 101n
Philosopher, Socrates the sole true one the world has known, 54; depicted in *Theaetetus,* 54 f.; the lesson of Socrates, 55; education of the elite should fall upon, 58; improbability of becoming chief of State, 92
Philosopher-kings, 56; years of education: goal at age of fifty, 83; servants of the city, 85; represent contemplative science of the intellect, 88; *see also* Guardians
Philosophic dialogues, 1-7; *see also* Dialogues
Philosophy, the science of measure of values, 33; not same as science, 35; politics and, 53-70; political, formulated by Greeks, 53n; salvation can come only through: what it involves, 69; role in education of elite for public office, 81 ff.; only for the elite, 82; a medicine of the soul, 90n; why tyranny attracts men more, 104 f.; role of, in checking political and social decay, 107-11
Philosophy of enlightenment, 23n
Physical education, 78, 79
Piety, 58
Plato, dialogues, 1-52; philosophic, 1-7; perfection of form, profundity of thought: effect upon readers, 1; historians and critics reassuring, 2; literary talent, 4, 34; never mocks his readers, 4; master of the parody, 18; glorification of Socrates: their first meeting: abandonment of narrative style for simpler literary composition, 34; an aristocrat, son of Ariston, 53; Socrates' influence upon, 53, 70, 107; criticism of sophistics occupies half his work, 63 (*see also* Sophistics); preference for ethics of the past: not a reactionary, 63; brothers, 67; aim in establishing the Academy, 70; totally free from worship of the State, 71; education his primary preoccupation, 76; that philosophy not accessible to all, a constant doctrine of, 82; mission to which life devoted, 107; modernity of

political thought, 110; timely significance of message, 111
Pleasure and power, ideal of, 61; *see* Tyranny
Pleasures, 30 f.; the good and the superfluous, 99n, 100
Plutocracy, *see* Oligarchy
Polemarchus in *Republic*, 64n, 71n
Political and philosophical problems the same, 53, 57
Political and social decay, possibility of checking, 106 ff.
Political virtue, 12, 22
Politicians, professional, 64, 99n, 102
Politics, and philosophy, 53-70; Greek participation in, 53; the just city, 71-93; imperfect cities, 93-106; conclusion, 106-11; *see also* Cities; Government
Polus in the *Gorgias*, 65n
Possessions, private: denied to city's guardians, 85
Possessive instinct, 85
Power, absolute, 92n; justified by knowledge alone, 108
Power (Ferrero), 103n
Power and pleasure, ideal of, 61; *see* Tyranny
Power of the strong, sophist beliefs, 61 ff.
Powers, separation of: unity, 75
Pre-existence, myth of, 10
Prevision, 39
Prodicus, in the *Protagoras*, 18n, 61n
Propaganda, role of, 88n
Propertied classes in a democracy, 102
Protagoras, the, 17-33, 53; beautiful and amusing, 17; a literary masterpiece, 18
Protagoras the man, 19, 49, 61n; does not rise above the popular level, 22; social relativism, 23, 37 f.; *see also* Sophistics
Psychology, interdependence of social and individual, 72; the unconscious, 104n

Quality transformed by quantity, 67n

Reader-auditor, 5
Reading aloud, 35
Realities or "things," 26
Reasoning, 51
Relationism, criticism of, 45n
Relativism, social, 23, 38
Religious reform the first basis of education, 78
Remembrance of forgotten knowledge, 10, 16, 17
Reminiscence, theory of, 10
Republic, the, 6n, 15n; philosopher-king the basis of, 57; discussion on justice, 64n, 65; subtitle: whether primarily about justice or the city, 71; preoccupation with guardian, 75
Revolution, 95, 99; leaders, 98
Rhetoric, 20 f.
Rights, natural, 61, 65n

Saintliness, 26; *see* Justice
Schelling, 5n
Science, not learned but invented by the soul, 7; the only thing that can be taught, 11; real thinking is what constitutes, 15; method of the Platonic dialectic that of, 15n; virtue found to be, 17, 18; as nourishment for the soul, 21; of the measure of values, 26 ff., 32; nature of, the problem dealt with in *Theaetetus*, 33-52; and philosophy, two separate things, 35; identification with true opinion, 40 ff.; linked with reasoning, 44, 49; nothing other than possession of truth, 50
Science of government, teaching of, 22n
Sensationalism, 37 ff., 48
Separation of powers, 75
Shakespeare, 5n
Slave, in the *Meno*, 8
Social and political decay, possibility of checking, 106 ff.
Social conformism, 12n, 13, 24
Social contract, theory of, 68, 73
Social hypocrisy, 66, 68

Index

Social relativism, 23, 38
Social science, teaching of, 22n
Socrates, questions propounded by, 1; doctrine, 2, 4, 6; why he occupies central position in the dialogues: ironic character of his ignorance, 3; his irony; companions at deathbed, 33; recalled and glorified in introduction to *Theaetetus*, 34; interest in, and influence upon, youth, 34, 37; condemnation and death of, determined philosophical life of Plato, 53; why condemned to death, 54 ff.; the world's sole true philosopher: undying influence, 54; the lesson of, 55; set up as the model statesman, 57; identification of justice with righteousness, the goal of, 65; belief that nobody commits evil voluntarily, 68n; task bequeathed by: shouldered by Plato, 70; error in addressing the masses only, and not the elite, 70n; education of city begun by, 107
Socratic dialogues, *see* Dialogues
Socratism and sophistics, 19 ff., 64
Soldiers, *see* Warriors
Solidarity the ultimate basis of city, 102n
Sophistics and Socratism, 19 ff., 64
Sophistics of Protagoras and followers, 12, 13n, 18 ff.; compared to the "philosophy of enlightment," 23n; a main basis of their teaching, 28n; rhetorical method, 29n; education, ideals, aims, 60 ff.; Plato's criticism of, occupies half his work, 63; tyranny inseparable from: essential opposition between Socratism and sophistics, 64; social philosophy repudiated by Plato's just city, 71; why wrong in social philosophy, 102n
Soul, thought its dialogue with itself, 3n, 40, 41n, 49; science nourishment for, 21; tripartite, 90, 105
Sparta, 76, 94n, 95, 96n, 97
Spectator-auditor, 4 f.
Spinoza, 24, 91n
State, Plato free from worship of, 71; characterized by unity and cohesion, 99; *see also* City
Statesman, the true, 15, 17, 57, 108; Athenian, condemned, 57; never to be confused with demagogue, 111
Statesman, the, 15n, 90n, 91n, 108
Stoics, 54, 91n
Strong, rights of the: sophist belief in, 61 ff.
Superfluous desires, 99
Syracuse venture, 70

Temptation, tests by, 81
Terpsion, companion of Socrates, 33, 34, 50
Thales, 55n
Theaetetus, the, 33-52; Dies's edition of, 37n; excerpt, 54
Themistocles, 12
Theodorus of Cyrene, in the *Theaetetus*, 33, 35, 48
"Things" or realities, 26
Thought, the soul's dialogue with itself, 3n, 40, 41n, 49; thinking constitutes science, 15; presupposes a passion for truth, 16
Thrasymachus, 64, 71n, 104n; political doctrine, 65 ff.
Thucydides, 12, 59n
Timaeus, the, 6n
Timocracy, or the city of courage and honor, 94-97, 109
Timocratic man, 95
Tripartite soul, 90, 105
Truth, 21, 50
Tyranny, the ideal of pleasure and power, 61 ff.; Plato on guard against: indissolubly joined with sophistics, 64; the perverted city of fear and crime, 94, 102-4; why it attracts men, 104 f.; reality of its menace, 106
Tyrant, can come from lower class, 98n; as "protector of the people," 103; a prey to fear, its effects, 103 f.

Unconscious, the, in man, 104n
Unity of State implies unity of power and command, 75

Index

Unity of the particularizations of one essence, 25
University, Academy the first, 70

Valéry, 5
Valor, equivalent of ancient "virtue" (*q.v.*), 8*n*
Values, the science of measure of, 26 ff., 32
Virtue, meaning of, and whether it can be taught, as discussed in *Meno*, 7-17; in *Protagoras*, 17-33; difference in their situations, 18; sense in which used by ancients, 8*n*; political, 12, 22; attempt to determine connections between virtue and the virtues, 25-29; popular notions concerning, 24; as knowledge, 29 ff.
Virtuous literature, 78, 79*n*

Warrior class, 74
Warriors, guardians like an ascetic order of, 87*n*, 91
Wealth, and its effects, 75; all forms denied city's guardians, 85; pursuit of, 97; not luxury, traits of oligarchic city, 98*n*
Whole and parts, relationship, 25
Will and intelligence, 81*n*
Women, not excluded from public life: planned education, 76; communal status, 85

Xenophon, 2, 7

Youth, dialogue written for, 19; Socrates' interest in, and influence upon, 34, 37; philosophy not for, 47, 82; training of, Plato's primary preoccupation, 76